Big Dreams, Daily Joys

Big Dreams, Daily Joys

SET GOALS. GET THINGS DONE.
MAKE TIME FOR WHAT MATTERS.

Elise Blaha Cripe

CHRONICLE BOOKS
SAN FRANCISCO

Library of Congress Cataloging-in-Publication Data available.

ISBN 978-1-4521-7654-3

Manufactured in China.

10 9 8 7 6 5 4

Chronicle Books LLC
680 Second Street
San Francisco, CA 94107
www.chroniclebooks.com

Design by Kelley Galbreath.

For my parents

(of course!)

Contents

LET'S GO!

3

Let's Dream Bigger

GET GOALS ON PAPER

4

Let's Get
It Done

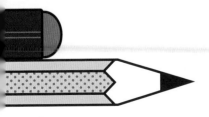

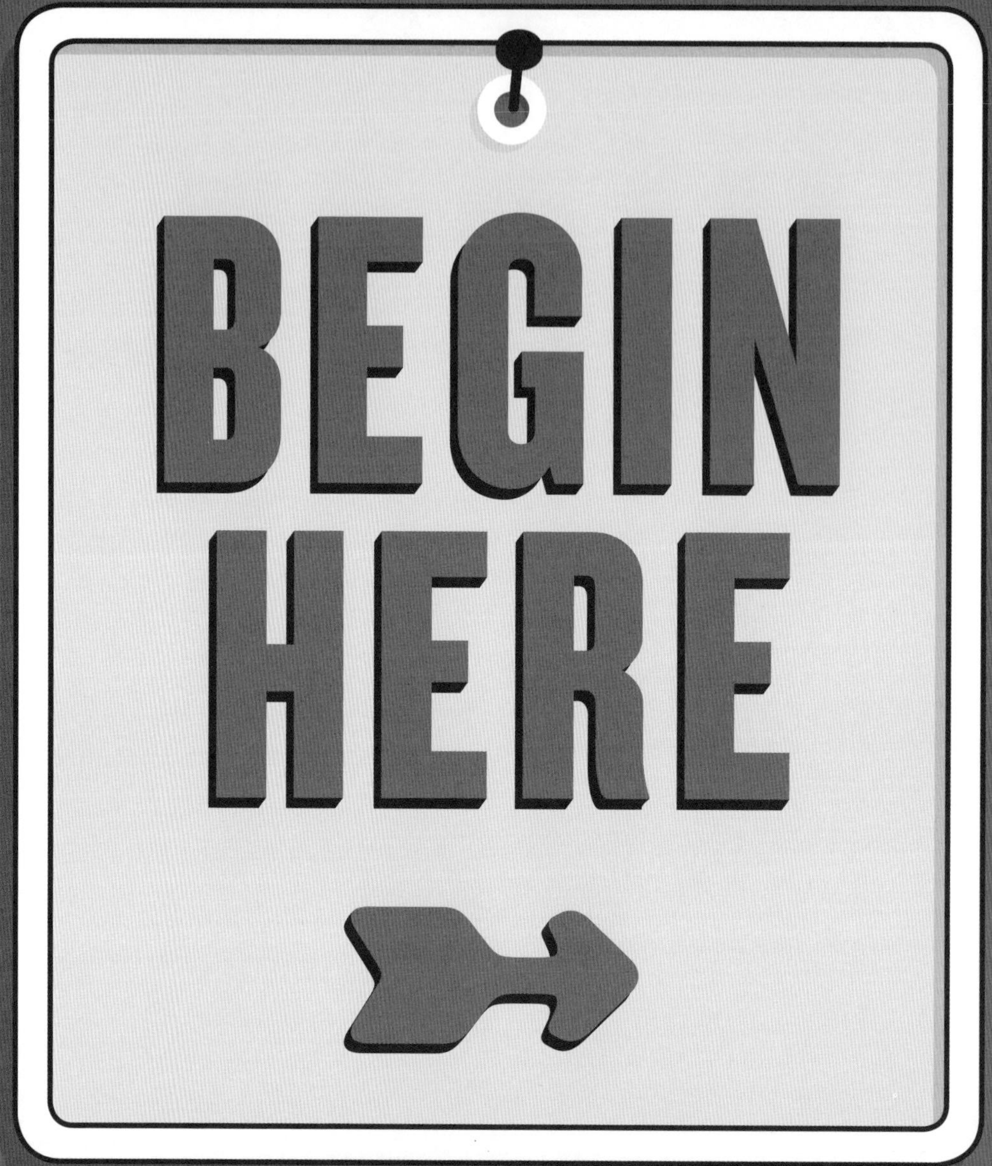
BEGIN
HERE

Here we go!

I USED TO DREAD BEING ASKED what I did for a living. I'd meet someone new and prepare myself for those five little words: "So . . . what do you do?"

I envied accountants, engineers, and food critics. It wasn't that I actually wanted any of those jobs. I didn't want to file other people's taxes. I didn't want to build bridges. I actually wouldn't have minded eating at fancy restaurants, but I didn't want to write about it. I just loved how simple those careers were to explain. I thought it would be nice to have a compact and concrete answer that described how I spent my days.

From the time I was in high school through my early twenties, I had worked jobs with concrete titles. I had been an activities director at a nursing home. I was a smoothie maker at Jamba Juice. I was an admissions office intern at the University of Southern California. I was a management intern at Target stores. I spent time interning as an insurance claims adjuster and a public relations team member. I was a sales associate and then a workshops coordinator and then an assistant manager at a craft and gift store called Paper Source.

All those positions were well defined. They were clear on paper and easy to say. They were jobs that seemed interesting enough, paid me every two weeks, and promised the "experience" I craved for my resume. None of them felt like the right fit, but they were something to do until I found what it was that I really wanted to be doing.

For the past nine years, I have been working for myself, and I am still trying to get comfortable with the "What do you do?" question. (That's a great side benefit of writing *Big Dreams, Daily Joys*. Now if asked, I'll be able to say, "I'm an author," and most people will get it.)

Part of why I have struggled so much with my answer is that what I do is always changing. For years I wrote daily blog posts. I opened an Etsy shop and sold letterpress prints and mini journals. I taught online classes. I designed a scrapbooking kit. I created and sold rubber stamps. I started a podcast. In 2014, when I couldn't figure out what to do next, I launched a project called MAKE29, and for a year I made it my job to create limited editions of various products such as knitted blankets, paintings, and screen-printed posters. I hoped that by the end of the year I would know what direction to take my business.

Another reason the "What do you do?" question gave me pause is that I never considered myself an expert or "professional enough" at anything I was doing. Each time I started something new, there was a similar pattern: my interest was piqued, I did a quick Google search for a tutorial or to research supplies, and then I hopped into the arena, ready to learn by doing. Who was I to call myself a writer? Or a designer? Or a podcaster? These were things that I was trying, sure, but what did I actually do to make a living and generate income? *I pieced together a bunch of ideas and hoped for the best.*

It took me years of piecing together "all the things" to find the "one thing" that finally felt right. In August 2014, while staining wooden plant stands with my dad to sell for my MAKE29 project, it hit me. "What if I sold a planner? A paper planner that had goal-setting features? What if instead of just talking about how to get stuff done, I gave people a tool that would help them do the stuff?"

"Now there's an idea," he said.

It was an idea. And it was the beginning of my current business and the first concept that felt like something I could do for a long time.

I launched Get To Work Book, my planner business, in the spring of 2015. I spent eight months and $45,000 turning an idea I'd had in my garage into a website ready to collect pre-orders. I was terrified.

People took a chance on my simple black-and-white planner and unofficial-looking website. Thanks mostly to social media and word-of-mouth recommendations, the Get To Work Book brand has grown. Today, my planner business is just over four years old and has fifty products under its umbrella. I lease a warehouse near my house and go there a few times a week to pack orders that are shipped all over the world. I got to turn my idea into a real business that helps people get stuff done.

This book is not about that one idea. It's not about how I started a billion-dollar company with five thousand employees and a #goals message (which is good because I don't have any of those things). It's not about how to get rich quick (you can't) or find your calling (you try everything you can) or hack a productive life in three simple steps (would you actually want to do that?).

Instead, this book is a guide to creating room in your days, dreaming bigger, and making progress toward your goals. It's about recognizing that through routine and pockets of time you can make progress and build a life you enjoy. This book will help you determine your priorities and show you how to separate the real work from the unnecessary fluff. I'll talk about making the most of your time by finding motivation, developing a practical schedule, and staying on track. And then I will share goal-reaching techniques that actually work and show you how to dream bigger.

Hours after I decided to write this book, I shared my intent with the internet. I am a big believer in making bold statements (we'll get into that later), and telling people what I am planning to do is part of how I turn my goals into action. A few minutes after I posted I got a message: "I would love to know when you knew you had become expert enough to write a book on a topic?"

Ahhhhhhh, I thought. *Finally a question scarier than "So . . . what do you do?" Is it too soon to give up?*

This book is a guide to creating room in your days, dreaming bigger, and making progress toward your goals.

Yep. Too soon. And also too late. I was going to write this. So my response was, "Great question. I am *not* an expert at goal-setting, but I am a lifelong explorer of this topic and I am excited to share what I have learned so far."

I am not an expert on getting stuff done or accomplishing goals, but I do get stuff done, and I have accomplished many of my goals. I know this terrain. I know where to start. I have learned what to avoid and what should be explored more fully. I have developed habits that work and tricks to try, whether you're overwhelmed with ideas or struggling to simply get one thing accomplished each day.

This book, like a hammer or a paper planner, is just a tool. It's not a magic wand or a guarantee that your life will change. If I have done my job right, it will serve as inspiration and give you something solid to jump off of, but ultimately *you* are going to do the work.

You will try new things. You will experiment and see what connects best for your schedule and dreams. You will make a difference in your own life.

Sound good? I hope so. Let's go. ➤➤

You will try
You will exp
and see wha
best for you
and dreams
make a diffe
your own lif

new things.
eriment
t connects
r schedule
You will
rence in
.

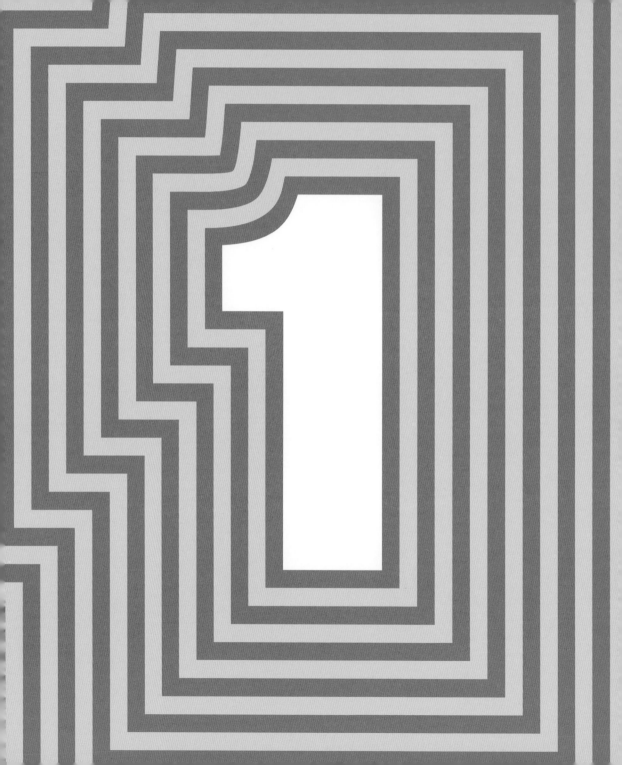

**IN THIS SECTION
I WILL**

- explain why goal-setting is so valuable
- separate everything you do into three layers
- share what makes a good goal
- encourage you to think like a child and a juggler
- recommend that you cultivate a healthy FOFSED (and tell you what it stands for!)
- hopefully help you see you're already ready to make some big changes

Part 1

Let's Get Started

We set goals to learn, expand, and find the joy that comes from getting uncomfortable and pushing ourselves outside the daily routine.

Why set goals?

I HAVE BEEN ACTIVELY SETTING and working toward various business and personal goals my entire adult life. Goal-setting enabled me to quit my day job and start my own creative ventures. It kept me upbeat and inspired during my husband's two deployments and helped me find my footing as an overwhelmed new mom. And it continues to keep me challenged and inspired to this day. Goal-setting has been the common thread in my work for more than a decade.

When I bring up goal-setting, I often watch people's eyes glaze over. They think either "boring" or that it's just about hype and Pinterest-ready quotes about "following your dreams." They reference an article about how New Year's resolutions tend to fail or share how they wish goal-setting worked for them.

But personalized, well-developed goals are anything but boring and are so much more substantial than an inspirational poster. They can encourage and motivate you to try new things, help you move forward after setbacks, and give you larger purpose in your daily life.

I have set goals for many reasons over the years. I wanted to improve. I wanted to change direction. I wanted to recover. I wanted to avoid boredom or stop feeling overwhelmed. I wanted to save money or make money. I wanted to slow time or get through what felt like a long season. I wanted to learn something new or apply a skill I already had. Overall, I wanted a challenge. I was ready to add something extra to my life.

The act of setting a goal is important, but on its own it's meaningless. You don't decide to try something and *boom!* your life is changed. But working toward a goal—even a goal that never gets fully realized—is where the magic happens. When you seriously commit and put forth effort, you will change and grow, regardless of whether you finish what you set out to do.

And that's what this is about. We set goals to learn, expand, and find the joy that comes from getting uncomfortable and pushing ourselves outside the daily routine.

What's the **difference** between goals and to-do-list items?

LET'S DEFINE these two important terms.

A goal **is something you work toward over a period time.** It might be a month. It might be a year. It might be twelve years. It's an objective that might be complicated and usually involves more than just a few steps. You could need training or to save money or to work with a team to accomplish a goal.

A to-do-list item **is something that you can get done in less than an hour.** It's a task. A single duty that has a start and stop time. You know when you've started and you know when you have finished.

You may have a lot on your to-do list and you may have a list of goals, but they are not the same thing. Let's explore this a bit further . . .

Everything that you do can be separated into three layers.

1 **LAYER 1 IS THE NECESSITIES.** You breathe. You eat. You sleep. These are the basics you need to do in order to live. Most likely, if you're reading this right now,

these are things you do every day without thinking too much about them (unless, of course, they are interrupted by an extenuating outside factor, and then they are *the only thing* you think about).

2 **LAYER 2 INCLUDES THE ACTIONS YOU PERFORM OVER AND OVER AGAIN TO SUSTAIN A NORMAL LIFE.** I am generalizing, but this would include everything from putting gas in the car to showering to taking out the trash to going to work. I would consider these the chores or habits that happen over and over again. Many of these things are so integral to your routine that you do them once a day or when they are needed without thinking much about them.

Layers 1 and 2 include everything that must be accomplished by you or someone in your household. They are not exciting, but they are, for the most part, necessary.

3 **LAYER 3 IS THE BONUS STUFF.** It's the more creative, more life-enriching (as opposed to life-sustaining) stuff that we

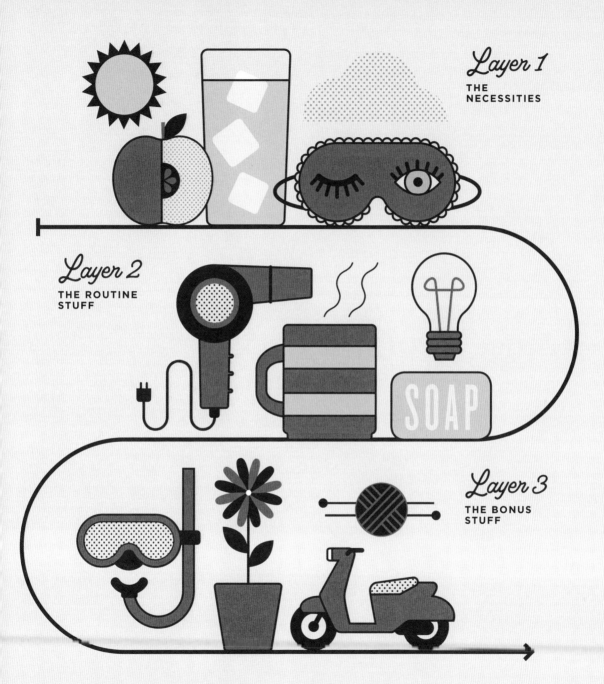

Layer 1
THE NECESSITIES

Layer 2
THE ROUTINE STUFF

Layer 3
THE BONUS STUFF

1
Layer 1
keeps us
alive.

2
Layer 2
keeps us
functioning.

3
Layer 3
brings the
joy.

choose to add to layers 1 and 2. For the most part, goal-setting and the majority of goals you will probably set will fall into the layer 3 category.

Layer 3 is where the creative experiments, challenging work projects, and magic are made. These are the things that come after the day-to-day activities, things that you want to add to your life because they make you feel happier and give you something to look forward to. Layer 3 is where hobbies happen. You don't have to do the layer 3 items, and that's what makes them exciting goals to work toward.

So how do goals and to-do-list items relate?

Layer 3 (the goal-setting portion of your activities) is made up of to-do-list items. All of your big goals can be broken down into smaller, more manageable steps, and this is an essential part of the goal-setting process. *If you don't break big goals up into actionable items, they serve as nothing more than wishes and will not be accomplished.*

We are going to talk much more about this in part 3, but keep it in mind. Goals are bigger concepts and may take a while to complete. To-do-list items are small, actionable items and should be things you can cross off after an hour or less of working.

It's also important to note that to get to layer 3 and begin to work on those fun and experimental projects, we have to make sure that everything on the first two layers is under control and well cared for. Part 2 of this book will cover organizing your daily tasks and managing your routine.

What makes a "good" goal?

GOOD GOALS ARE MEANINGFUL, inspiring, possible, measurable, and explainable.

Meaningful: Your goal should be important to you. It should be something that you care about accomplishing. Ideally, the purpose will come from you, not the promise of someone else's validation. This goal should matter enough for you to sacrifice your extra time and give it the respect it deserves.

Inspiring: Your goal should feel a bit out of your grasp right now. It should be something to reach for, not something you can just cross off (that's a to-do-list item). You will need to stretch or jump or try in order to meet this goal. It's going to take effort to achieve.

Possible: Your goal should be doable. Not today. Maybe not even next year. But someday. To be realistic, this goal should be something that you can achieve. There is no point in setting a goal to be six feet tall if you're five feet four and haven't grown in ten years.

Measureable: Your goal should be some thing you can track. It should be concrete, and you should know when you are making progress. "Be happy" is a great mantra and it's something to strive for, but can you be more specific? What makes you happy? What activities help you feel happy? What lifestyle changes can you implement to increase your happiness? Form a measurable goal around those things.

Explainable: Your goal should be explainable via text message. It should be simple to say—even if it will not be simple to reach. A good goal can be communicated in a sentence. Try building off of one of these:

I am _____
_____.

I will _____
_____.

I am going to _____
_____.

Keep it simple. Make it meaningful. Be sure you can measure it and that it's doable. And then reach for it.

Stop waiting until you're "ready"

CHOOSING A GOAL that connects and makes sense for you is the first step. After that you must give yourself permission to start working toward this goal. For many people, this is the much harder task. We tend to give up before we even start something because we fear we are unprepared to do it. Here's the bad news: you *are* unprepared to do something before you've done it. Here's the good news: *that doesn't matter.*

Expertise, perfection, and inspiration are all great, but in most situations (open-heart surgery and high government positions excluded) they can be overrated and act more like hurdles than trampolines. Making the most of your days and making progress on goals is about learning as you go, embracing imperfection, and showing up to do the work. This is good. It means, whether you believe it or not, that you already have what you need to get started. You're in the exact right place to begin.

You learn how to do something by trying. You can read a book (do that!). You can take a class (sign up!). But ultimately, it's only by *doing the thing* that you learn the thing.

This means that if we waited until we knew how to do something before we attempted it, we would never do anything.

This "learn by trying" experience is something that comes naturally to children. I have two daughters. Watching them grow and develop skills is one of the greatest joys of my life. When my older daughter, Ellerie, was learning to walk, I saw "learn by doing" in action. It was a scary three months between the first time she pulled up to stand and when she took those initial wobbly steps. It was tedious and at times painful, but it was also the most awesome and literal example I can think of where someone just put one foot in front of the other.

Ellerie didn't wait until she was an expert or had mastered walking before she tried walking. She learned by doing. There were many, many failed attempts until finally—success!

The way we learned to walk is the way we learn everything. We watch. We pay attention. But then we do it. *We try the thing.*

The other great lesson we can take from kids is that when they learn something new, they don't expect it to be hard. Their memories are shorter, and so there isn't a story playing in their heads warning them that this is going to be difficult. As adults, we tend to think that because we struggled with X, Y will be hard. Kids, on the other hand, don't compare new pursuits to past

Here's the bad news: you are unprepared to do something before you've done it.

Here's the good news: *that doesn't matter.*

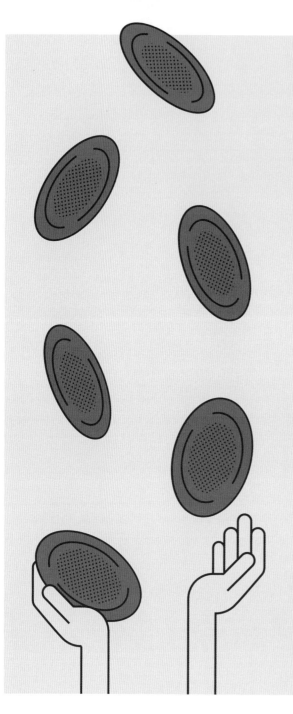

Try This
Be like a juggler

HAVE YOU EVER WATCHED SOMEONE juggle? They don't throw all the plates in the air at once and hope for the best. They throw one plate. Then two. Then three. Then, maybe, they add more. It's impressive to watch ("Look how many things they have in the air!"), but when you look closer, you see that while they are aware of each item, they are actually handling *just one or two things at any moment.*

This is how you should add new projects and tasks to your life: one thing at a time. Do you find your layer 1 and layer 2 tasks easy to maintain? (If not, don't worry, we'll cover that soon.) If so, consider adding something else. Get really comfortable throwing that *one* new plate in the air. Then add another. Take your time adding that second plate. Can you do this? Can you keep two plates up with energy to spare? Great. Add a third plate and toss just those three things until you once again feel comfortable and capable.

You cannot start with multiple ideas and projects at the same time and expect to find success with all of them. You'll fail. And worse than that, you'll be overwhelmed and discouraged because without your undivided focus and attention it's unlikely any of the new things you try will work. Take your time and add things to your life with purpose. It may be a year before you can get that second plate in the air, but when you do, you'll know that the first plate won't come crashing down.

experiences. They don't know how long this is supposed to take or how difficult it might turn out to be. As a result they are naive, impatient, and easily frustrated. But you know what else? They are confident, adventurous, and ready to go. We can learn so much from this.

Over the years I have tried many things both as hobbies and as professional projects. At the start of each, I didn't know what to do. Before I tried, I had no experience sewing or quilting or growing vegetables or designing rubber stamps or producing a planner. But *because* I tried so many new projects, I had plenty of experience being a beginner. I knew that at the start of whatever I was about to attempt I would know nothing, and that it would be okay. I would have to Google suppliers. I would have to consult video tutorials. I would have to ask for help. I would have to make mistakes. I would have to start over. I would have to be uncomfortable. That's how it works.

You will most likely not be "ready" on day one to try something new. You will need to start anyway. If you're waiting for someone to give you permission, I'm giving it to you right now.

You will most likely not be "ready" on day one to try something new. You will need to start anyway. If you're waiting for someone to give you permission, I'm giving it to you right now.

Nobody knows what they are doing

ONE OF THE REASONS YOU MIGHT FEAR you are not ready is that you see others doing what you want to be doing and they seem so confident. Your inner monologue tells you, *Surely they have it all figured out. Surely they know how to do this. Surely they started with more tools and more knowledge than I have.*

Your inner monologue is wrong. Those people? They are figuring it out just like you are. They made a decision to learn and they started. They may be further along than you, but they are struggling with their own doubt and insecurity, and most days they are continuing to put one foot in front of the other anyway (and some days they are finding themselves backtracking and starting over). They are making it up as they go. The only difference between you and them is that they have been doing this longer and therefore have more experience troubleshooting and getting back up after they fall down.

But to really move forward and make progress on your own path, it's not enough to just know that other folks hit stumbling blocks or (of course!) are flawed. You need to put your head down and stop measuring yourself against others. The internet has brought vast numbers of people, ideas, and stories to us, which can be both good and bad. It's aspirational ("Look what's possible!") and terrible ("Look at all the things I'll never do and will never have!"). It's brought to our fingertips a world of inspiration and a world of opportunity for comparison.

I hear people talk about their FOMO (fear of missing out) a lot. I hope I suffer from the much-less-catchy "FOFSED." *Fear of following someone else's dreams.* When you are always looking around and comparing yourself to others, it's easy to forget what actually matters to you. It's confusing, and you can start down a path that doesn't make any sense for who you are or where you are in life.

Years ago I stumbled across a globe-trotting family on Instagram. After scrolling through their feed I started to feel as if my husband and I needed to quit our jobs, sell our house, pack up the kids, and hit the road. It took me half a day of feeling unsettled to remember that my husband has years left on his Navy commitment, we love our house, and ultimately . . . I am a homebody, and extended travel makes me anxious. I could follow this family's photos and admire their adventures, *but I didn't have to change my life or my idea of what creates "happiness" for me.*

Maybe you can relate? Have you found yourself going further than admiring what someone has or is doing and wanting to jump into that life? Do you find that you're so fearful of missing out on something else that you can't commit to anything? In these times it's valuable to get clear about what you are working toward. If you know what your dream is and can set your expectations around that, it's much easier to stay focused.

Before we get into how to make the most of the days you have, it's crucial that you acknowledge that *who you are* and *what you are doing* is valuable. As you develop and maintain a realistic workflow and then start moving toward new goals, your focus has to be on yourself, not on what those around you appear to be doing. You're not going to be able to do everything perfectly, but you will be able to do some things really well. That's good. It's more than good; it's enough.

You're not going to be able to do everything perfectly, but you will be able to do some things really well. That's good. It's more than good; it's enough.

EXACTLY ENOUGH

You Are OK

Goals are about getting results— yes—but working *toward* your goals is the best part of this process. If we are lucky, we will get to spend a lifetime engaged creatively, mentally, and physically.

So let's get started

THIS BOOK ISN'T A FOUR-STEP PLAN to greatness or a foolproof "do the most stuff" guide. The concepts here are about creating a daily lifestyle and attitude that is manageable and brings you joy. Goals are about getting results—yes—but working *toward* your goals is the best part of this process. If we are lucky, we will get to spend a lifetime engaged creatively, mentally, and physically. If we are lucky, we will get to continue to work toward things that are important to us.

Over the years, I have checked off a lot of my personal and business goals. The satisfaction of that checkmark is great, but it's *nothing* compared to the joy of starting something new, learning what works, finding new methods, and problem-solving my way to the finish line. Those are the moments I remember when I think back on the past decade. That's why I do this. I set goals not to collect completed checkmarks or to hang up "I did it!" medals. Instead, I do this to enrich my daily life through projects, experiences, and work that I enjoy.

I want to show you that you have enough time for the things that matter to you. I want to encourage you to take that first step toward a big dream. To do that, we need to clear some space and time in our days. ➡➡

Part 2

Let's Make Room for Joy

The point of planning isn't to schedule every moment of our days. The point of planning is so we *don't* have something to do every moment of our days.

Why plan?

THE POINT OF PLANNING isn't to schedule every moment of our days. We plan so that we can stay on track. We plan so that we can get ahead. We plan so that we can maintain focus. We plan so that when things go awry it's not the end of the world. We plan so setbacks don't destroy everything we have built. We plan in order to build space into and around our lives and work.

Ultimately, the point of planning is so we *don't* have something to do every moment of our days.

"Planning" looks different for everyone. I wish I could say, "*This. Do this.* You'll be set forever." People would be thrilled. A single solution to a complicated problem? I'd be rich. But of course it's not like that. You have to experiment with planning. You have to try some different methods. You have to be open to change. You also have to be willing to do some work.

In the following pages I'll give you some tips on how to jump-start your daily schedule, and then you can experiment until you find the methods that work for you.

Why are you not getting things done?

NOT GETTING THROUGH your daily to-do list is normal. We've all been there. You have a list at the start of the day. The day ends and your list still has things left on it. You didn't finish everything. No big deal; it's normal. Tomorrow comes. You move yesterday's tasks to today's list, plus you add a few. Tomorrow ends. You didn't finish. No big deal; it's normal.

Yep! It's normal. *But it's also a cycle that you can break*. I would argue it's essential that you break it in order to carve out extra time in your day and your life for the "bonus" layer 3 things you *want* to be working on.

There are three reasons why you don't get your to-do-list items accomplished: lack of time, lack of communication, or lack of interest.

Sometimes a schedule change leaves you without enough time. Sometimes a communication error means you didn't get what you needed from another person in order to check something off your list. And sometimes lack of interest in a project means you felt unmotivated and procrastinated or pushed it off.

That's it. There are only three reasons for why you didn't complete something you wanted

or needed to do by the end of the day. To help you identify the issue that's preventing you from completing the task at hand, ask yourself the following questions:

- *What's going wrong here that's preventing me from getting this done?*

- *Where can I get more time to work on this?*

- *Who can I contact to help me with this?*

- *What deadline needs to be communicated so I can move forward?*

- *Am I sure I'm really interested in doing this?*

And then, most important:

- *What's going to change tomorrow or next week or next month that's going to allow me to accomplish this?*

These questions are worthwhile because they simplify the all-consuming problem of "I can't get

Why Didn't You GET IT DONE?

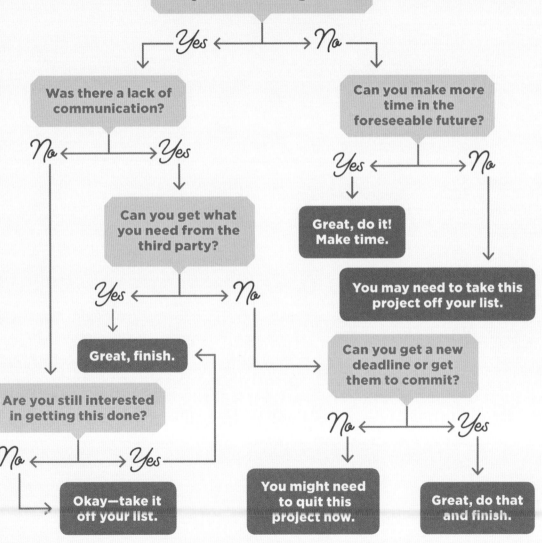

this done." They take an abstract feeling of being stuck and illuminate the real issue so that you can begin fixing it. This is a valuable exercise, but it's important that you don't judge the results or your answers. Evaluate the reason, and then determine if there is a fix. Don't get upset over your lack of time or berate yourself for not having enough motivation. If you start to associate negative feelings with this reflection process, you will be less inclined to do it again and will continue to make the same mistakes.

This is about improving and hopefully stopping the "I'll do that tomorrow" cycle. If you want something to change, *you must change the situation.*

Why write things down?

YOU MAY ALSO STRUGGLE to accomplish your tasks because you don't know what you need to do.

If you are already a dedicated list-maker and love your process, please skip right ahead to the next section. But if not: Hi! Let's chat. I know I said I can't tell you exactly how to get things done or to be more productive each day, but I can tell you this: *you need to start writing things down.*

Writing down your tasks for the week or day is valuable for many reasons. Here are three of the biggest ways lists can improve your time management:

A list creates space: Once you get something down on paper, you can temporarily clear it from your mind. You can spend your mental energy on other tasks that involve problem-solving or creative thinking. Once your tasks are in writing, your to-do list doesn't need to be a persistent thought in the back of your mind because your paper (or device) is remembering it for you.

A list helps you sort: When tasks and ideas are out of your head and you can see them all in one place, it becomes easier to assess what you need to accomplish. You may already have a good sense of how long certain tasks take, so once you write them down, you can determine in which order to tackle them based on how much time you have.

A list saves time: A list is easy to refer to when you do find yourself with some time. You will not have to waste those free minutes trying to figure out what needs to be done. Your list already knows. It's there, waiting to help you get started.

How you decide to keep your list is up to you. I use a paper planner (obviously, it's my job), but that's not the only way to stay organized. An inexpensive spiral notebook works. A sticky note works. An app works. An online calendar works. My only caution with going digital for your list-making is that there are a lot of digital distractions. I don't use an app because if I did, every time I looked at my phone to see what I had to do, there would be twenty other apps calling for my attention. That's not helpful.

Why prioritize?

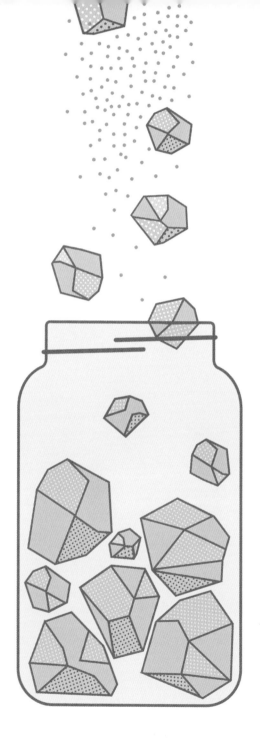

ANOTHER REASON WHY your "list of things" can feel overwhelming even once written down is that you are unable to separate the priorities from nonessential or non-urgent tasks. You may see a to-do list but not have a good idea of which item is the "most important" and therefore not give yourself the necessary time for what matters most.

One way to visualize your priorities and time is through the rock jar concept. Let's say you have five large rocks (your priorities), twenty smaller rocks (smaller tasks), and a pile of sand (frivolous to-dos) that all need to fit into a jar (your week). If you put the sand in first, the jar is too full to add the large rocks and all the smaller rocks. If you put the small rocks in first, you can't fit all the larger rocks. But if you put the larger rocks in first, then the smaller rocks will fill in around them. Last, you add the sand, which will slip its way into the extra space that remains.

There is room in your days for the items you have to complete. Prioritizing is about paying attention to the order in which you address them.

Determining
your priorities

ONE METHOD FOR FIGURING OUT what is actually a priority is to step back and look further ahead. What do you *have to get done* this month? Write those things down. What would you *like to get done* this month? Add those things to the list, too. You may have only three things. You may have twelve. Don't overthink this list; just jot down what comes to mind.

Then at the beginning of each week, refer back to your master or monthly list and pick two or three things that you want to get done during the next week. Some of these items might be single-task actions (such as scheduling a dentist appointment), while some may be more involved (such as packing up your house to move).

The point, regardless of the actions, is that on Monday, when the new week starts, *you already know what your main things to be accomplished are*. You know that you need to make that phone call or that you need to dedicate three days to packing up the house. These are your priorities and they are set in stone, regardless of what else appears in your email inbox this week or whatever idea pops into your head in the shower.

You can still add those email tasks to your list. You can still be excited over that new shower idea. *But these new additions cannot be your first focus this week*. You already know what you have to get done because you have set your priorities in advance.

This exercise suggests looking at a month first and then at weeks within that month. You may find that schedule too frequent for you (if so, try looking at a year or a quarter and then coming up with monthly priorities). Or you may find that weekly priorities are not enough to keep you focused (if that's the case, at the end of each day think about your first few priorities for the next day).

As with anything, you will have to experiment to see what works best for you and your schedule. This prioritization method might feel uncomfortable at first, and that's okay. It can be difficult to focus or re-focus when you are used to multitasking or charging ahead without much of a plan. It is worth doing though. Prioritizing your tasks is one small way that you can take control over your days and your time. You can draw a line and follow through on important tasks first, and so the other things can fall into place around it.

A second method for determining your priorities is to take a few minutes—*before* you sit down at your computer, or check your phone—to make a short list of what you need to get done today. Before you have seen a single distraction, what is on your list to accomplish? Taking a few minutes to answer this question can help you focus on what is going to be important for your day *before* outside requests start demanding your focus.

One thing I would caution you about this is to not determine your priorities too far ahead. A week at a time tends to be enough. If on January 1 you mapped out your weekly priorities for the next three months, you would most likely fall behind or get to March 5 and realize what you had planned isn't relevant anymore. Your focus(es) for the week should be manageable and realistic, and the closer you are to the time frame you're working with, the better you'll understand what is actually needed and what you can accomplish.

The three things concept

IN THE EARLY DAYS after Ellerie was born, I was in love with her but also exhausted, in pain, and overwhelmed. In order to stay sane, I was clinging to anything that resembled my old normal. To try and find that, every night I chose three things that I would get done the next day. Before going to bed, I wrote my to-do list.

In the beginning it was incredibly simple stuff. Send three thank-you notes. Wash a load of laundry. Deposit the check that came. Or schedule a follow-up doctor's appointment. Order more burp cloths. Upload photos.

Just three things. I had to get out of bed, shower, eat, nurse and change the baby, and complete three simple tasks. That was it. Those were my days. The point was not to actually get the thank-yous written or the clothes washed; the point was to re-establish normalcy. It was to feel the accomplishment of setting daily micro goals and crossing them off.

The new life goal—raise a human—I had just added to my plate was overwhelming. Parenthood felt immeasurable and vast those early weeks (honestly, it still does, but I am a bit more accustomed to it). In comparison, my simple to-dos were more manageable. Accomplishing these little things gave me a sense of satisfaction that buoyed me and allowed me to be better at my other, much larger tasks—healing and mothering.

Over time, things evened out and I returned to a more normal lifestyle. But the takeaway for me was how important focusing on just a few of the little things can be when the big things start to overwhelm. This exercise isn't just for new mothers. This is a technique you can try any time that things feel out of control or you feel out of practice making progress on your list.

Pick some small things that take just minutes and focus on only those items. You can do these small things, and these small things can lead to larger things.

Big-picture scheduling

KEEPING A LIST AND PRIORITIZING are the first two things you can do to take control of your time and schedule. The third is to create some organization in your schedule.

We all have different demands on our time, but they generally fall into three categories.

External Demands **are preset dates on the calendar:** holidays/celebrations, days on or off work/school, events/practices/meetings that someone else sets.

Negotiated Demands **are things that you have to schedule or attend, but you have some choice as to when they occur:** doctor's appointments, car tune-ups, dates, meetings you help set.

Internal Demands **are things that you want to enjoy or need to get done but can fit in at various times:** workouts, errands, hobbies, free time.

For the most part, the external and negotiated demands have to be added to your schedule first.

You can't change the date of Halloween or ask your child's school to stay open on President's Day because you have something else to do. You often have to work around business hours and with other people's schedules for negotiated demands, which can be constraining.

And often, once those two demands are entered into your calendar, there is limited time left for the internal demands you'd like to accomplish.

This can feel stressful. It's hard to watch events, meetings, and appointments pile up and see free time slipping away.

I invite you to accept it. This is your life. Start getting all those events organized. A paper planner works for this, a simple wall calendar works for this, an online calendar or app works for this. The point is you must be able to see the demands you've committed to. *You need to be able to see the space you don't have to find the space you do have.*

Once you know where you are already committed, it becomes easier to make commitments to yourself and schedule those internal demands. You'll see an hour-long window to go to the

NOVEMBER

Sunday	Monday	Tuesday	Wednesday	Thursday	Friday	Saturday
			1	2	3 **B**	4
C	6	7 **VOTE!** **A**	8	9	10	11
	13	14	15 **C**	16	17	18 Book club 7pm **B**
19	20	21 **C**	22	23 **A**	24	25
26	27 **B**	28	29 Meeting 3pm **B**	30		

A
External Demands
preset dates on the calendar

B
Negotiated Demands
**things that you have to
schedule or attend**

C
Internal Demands
**things that you want to enjoy
or need to get done**

grocery store or get out for a walk or tend to your garden. Knowing that you have that time—even if it's a fifteen-minute pocket—is encouraging and motivating. You have a reason to wrap things up at work quickly and get home. You know what you're going to do tonight after the kids are in bed. You can plan for those minutes of doing the things you love.

Getting organized is ultimately about becoming aware. You clean out your pantry to see what you are already storing and what you have to use. You sort your paperwork so you know where things are. You organize your calendar so that you can anticipate where there may be free space.

Getting organized is ultimately about becoming aware.

re-evaluating what's in your life

A BIG PART OF CREATING A SCHEDULE and seeing your calendar is evaluating everything on it. What are you actually doing? What do you need to do every month, week, and day? So often there are things on your list that you do out of habit or "because that's how it's always been done," but in reality these tasks are no longer necessary (or they can be simplified).

A few years ago I spoke with the author and artist Jason Kotecki about dealing with general life "overwhelm." He said something that stuck with me: "Let's opt out of the craziness and then mindfully opt in to the stuff that makes sense." Jason recommended looking at your life as an inbox. What did you actually sign up for, and what snuck in and is now just spam and noise? How can you unsubscribe from the stuff that is no longer necessary or helpful? How can you clear out some of that clutter?

Doing this means becoming an active participant in deciding what gets added to your life. It doesn't always feel like it, but you are in charge here. Whenever I talk about this sort of thing (I call it "choosing your actions") and suggest letting go of the stuff you hate, I get a comment about "hating doing the dishes" or "hating taking out the trash" and then a joking request for permission to stop doing those tasks. The commenter isn't serious, but what's interesting is that if you really want to, *you can* avoid this stuff. You can use paper plates and throw them away after each meal (please don't). You can reward your kid or spouse or neighbor for taking out your trash. There are options here, but when you think through them, it might make more sense to just do them yourself.

It's human nature to pick silly things to complain about *because* they are silly. It's easy to say, "I don't like [insert random chore here]," and make light of this statement. But to choose your actions seriously is to admit that you have control over many of the big things in your life that make you happy and unhappy. That's hard! If you admit that, you may have to make some changes. Often you are holding on to bad habits, unpleasant routines, or toxic relationships because you know what to expect with them. If you change them, you will be taking a step into the unknown. Again, that's hard. It's also a huge part of making room for joy.

Opt in

WRITE DOWN EACH OF YOUR COMMITMENTS, habits, activities, and tasks on small pieces of paper or index cards. Think both big and small, personal and work related. This could include PTA meetings, exercise classes, carpool driving, work obligations, TV shows you watch, podcasts you listen to, laundry, and so on. Be as specific as possible and write down everything you can think of that you do.

Step away from that list for a bit. Give yourself time to add to it (more ideas will come, I promise). Then with a clear head (and ideally when you're not tired), revisit your stack of cards.

Make two piles. One for the things you want to opt into and one for the things you would like to opt out of. Don't worry about the logistics or reality (yet). This is in an ideal world. What would you like to have in your life? What would you choose to unsubscribe from?

Look through your opt-in pile. What's there? Are you currently focusing on these important items? Do they feel like they are already constants in your life, or do you need to make some space for them? If it seems as if there are more than you have time for, that's okay. Save your opt-in pile. Pick one of the things in it that you would like more time for, and make a point over the next month to choose that item to work on when you find yourself with a few spare minutes or hours.

Next, look through your opt-out pile. Is there anything here that you can give up today? Like that TV show that you turn on out of habit but actually don't like anymore? What about bigger things? Are there projects you are half-heartedly working on? Is there a meeting you attend every month when you would rather be anywhere else? Can you let any of this stuff go? Of course there are some things that you can't opt out of right away, but next month or next year might be the right time to gracefully step down or move on.

The things that you commit to and the things that you do make up who you are. This exercise isn't about changing it all today or blowing up your life. It's also not about eliminating every single thing you don't like to do (we are all adults here). Instead, this is about realizing you are in control and getting clear on what you choose to do with your time. In making these piles, you are taking a small step toward adding in more of what you love and a step away from the stuff that you dread.

You need to be able to see the space you don't have to find the space you do have.

Building routine into your to-do list

AFTER THINKING ABOUT what you want to have on your list, the next step is to get that list in an order that flows with your daily life. Some activities make sense to do at certain times, and they're already such a part of your routine that you do them without even thinking about it. (You brush your teeth in the morning and before bed, for example.)

But nearly every activity you do should have a set time.

Take a few minutes to think about your days. When do you feel your most energetic? When do you have the most focus? When do you prefer to get out for a walk? Is there a time that the grocery store tends to be the emptiest? (Or maybe you like shopping when it's crowded and full of energy?)

I recently found a pocket of time to give my house a quick cleaning, and it's made a giant difference in my attitude. Every Sunday morning, my husband, Paul, takes the girls to Costco right when it opens. They are all out of the house for forty-five minutes to an hour, and this gives me just enough time to straighten up the rooms, clean the toilets, get a load of laundry in, clear the kitchen sink and countertops, and sweep the floor. I spring into action the moment that door shuts, and I am usually just finishing up when they burst back into the house with a week's worth of groceries.

This time works for two reasons. First, it's a dedicated opportunity to clean without little hands making new messes as I go, and second, it's a refresh at the start of the week. The house gets turned upside down on Saturday when we are all home together, and on Sunday morning I have a quick chance to rebalance before we turn it all upside down again.

When you pay attention to the flow of your days and weeks, you can match energy levels to activities. I like to write in the morning after I drop my girls off at school, in the afternoon after lunch, or right after I have cleared my email inbox. (I feel alert and free of distractions then.) I often pack shop orders in the afternoon when my eyes need a break from the computer. In the summer, I like to go for a walk in the evening after dinner and before we put the kids to bed. (It's a good way to get us out the house.) Before picking up my older daughter from school each weekday, I check email for the last time and then straighten up the kitchen and living room. I work from home, so this is an important transition period for me, when I can get the house back in order but also adjust my focus away from work and back to my role as a mom.

Having compartments for your daily tasks helps you feel more focused and can provide anchor points in your day and week. Remember, building schedules isn't about eliminating spontaneity. You are locking in solid time for activities to ultimately give yourself more unscheduled time. You're building a routine so you have time to break the routine.

You're building a routine so you have time to break the routine.

Finding pockets

THE NUMBER ONE QUESTION I am asked in response to a project or activity I've shared on social media is: "Where do you find the time to [insert thing I shared here]?" It comes up most frequently when I post a book recommendation.

So let's use reading as an example. Here's how I find "pockets" of time to read:

The first thing to note is that I love to read, which means it's high on my list of ways to fill my time. (If you don't, that's okay! You will want to use your pockets for something else that you enjoy.) The second thing is that I try to pick books that are engaging. I want to read a book that makes me forget I have a phone and doesn't take a ton of effort to "get into." (I will give up on books that don't connect with me quickly, guilt-free—life is way too short for stories you don't enjoy.)

I still read "real" paper books instead of using an e-reader. I found that if I read on an app, it was too easy to click on something else, and I didn't want to invite the distraction. I also prefer to read "real" books because I spend a lot of time reading in front of my girls. From their vantage point, if I read on my phone, tablet, or e-reader, it looks as if I'm just scrolling (which they see

me do plenty of already). If I am holding a paper book, it's clearer that I am reading, and that's an example I am happy to set for them.

When I share that I read a lot in front of my girls, people say, "But don't they interrupt you?" Of course! They are kids. They "interrupt" every bit of my life. But the more they see me reading, the more they get it. *Reading is a thing that Mama does, the same way that she brushes her teeth or checks her email or drives the car or plays with me or cooks mac and cheese or reads me a story. This is part of what Mama does and it's normal.*

In the beginning, whatever new thing you are trying to fit into a pocket of time isn't going to be "normal." It will feel difficult and you may be distracted or forgetful, but if you do something once and it doesn't go as expected or perfectly, you don't give up. You do it again, right?

I pick up my book in the morning while the kids watch a cartoon and eat their breakfast. I pick up my book while they splash in the bathtub, while they take swim lessons, while I am boiling water for spaghetti, and while they are playing in the backyard. I read while I wait for doctor's appointments or for a flight to take off.

Sometimes I get through three chapters in one sitting, and sometimes I read the same paragraph four times. I spend about 50 percent of my downtime reading, when I would otherwise pick up my phone. And that's enough. If just some of the time that you went to scroll through your phone you read instead (or did something else you value), you, too, would start getting through some books (or other activities you enjoy).

There are so many pockets in the day and you can put anything into them. You can choose what you love—watching cooking tutorials, gardening, training for a marathon. The most important thing here is recognizing that we get to choose how we fill this time. These minutes do not have to be forfeited to our phones.

Try this

Sort your tasks

GRAB A PIECE OF PAPER and divide it into three sections: morning, afternoon, evening. Write in each section the "logical" place for when you like to do daily activities. List everything you do. For example, when do you prefer to grocery shop? Go to the gym? Take a shower? Meditate? Watch TV?

This breakdown can become a guide for how you schedule your tasks. Experiment for a few days and see how this goes. What can you move around? What is working? What's not working? Do your activities match your energy? Can you move them around to build in more flow?

Honor your time zones

WHEN MY DAUGHTER WAS A TODDLER, I realized that throughout my day, I was living and working in two different time zones. There was "Elise Time" when I could be efficient and dig deep into projects. And then there was "Ellerie Time" when the clock slowed and everything took longer to accomplish.

I learned quickly that I could do anything on Elise Time, but I could also do many things on Ellerie Time. It was important that I used each zone appropriately. For example, I could unload the dishwasher by myself while Ellerie napped and it would take three minutes. Every dish went back in the right spot quickly and I was on to the next thing. Or, I could unload the dishwasher while Ellerie was awake and wanted to help. Every dish was unloaded but the process took closer to ten minutes, and my silverware looked like a disaster afterward.

But do you see what happened? In both cases, the dishes got put away. If I did it on Ellerie Time, it was an activity. We spent ten minutes together and did something that needed to get done. If it was on Elise Time, it was done, yes, but those three minutes could have been better spent on something I can't do with Ellerie's help (check my email, resew a hem, sit and drink my coffee in silence).

There are tasks that are part of my life that I don't need to bring into my personal time zone. I can do the laundry, work in the garden, grocery shop, fold clothes, make pizza dough, or handle hundreds of other chores while the girls "help." Sure, these tasks take longer in my daughters' time zone; I get interrupted, flour gets spilled, dirt gets thrown, but we still get it done.

You may not have kids, but your life still has time zones. Time may feel different when your partner or roommate is home. At work you may find that your most productive and focused hour is the first one before many of your coworkers have arrived for the day. Acknowledging and accepting the various time zones that exist in your house and office allows you to assign tasks to the right time of day. And it gives you a chance to really work (or play) when you're in *your* zone. Don't waste your "free time" on chores while you are in *your* zone! Spend that time doing the things that require your undivided attention and creative energy.

Alone
Time
ZONE 1

Family
Time
ZONE 2

Stop reinventing
the wheel

SOMETHING THAT HAS HELPED my daily schedule come together is establishing what works for me and then doing those same things over and over.

A few examples:

- **I take a lot of photos (for my job and just for fun) and I style my images one of four ways every time:** (1) straight down, (2) against a clean or fun background, (3) item partially cropped out of the frame, and (4) camera balanced on a flat surface with a "horizon" of the floor or table dividing the shot. That's it. Those are the only things I do and I repeat them because I like the look and it saves me from wondering how to "best" shoot something.

- **I have a black dress that I wear to almost every event.** Fancy dinner out with my husband? The dress with heels. Casual-ish dinner out with my family? The dress with flats. Dinner with my girlfriends? The dress. Dinner with the book club I haven't yet met? The dress. Work event? Play in the city? The dress. Always the dress. I love this dress. It fits, it's comfortable, it's flattering, it works. I have expanded on this so my whole closet is made up of simple staple pieces in a limited color palette that I either buy or sew. I like the "uniform" I have created for myself because it feels good and works for my lifestyle.

- **I review my email in the same way each time I open my inbox.** First I check the updates tab (bills to pay, receipts, shipping notifications). I make notes of anything that needs to be saved, add expenses to my spreadsheet, and pay any bills. I archive everything else. Second, I check my promotions tab, which includes email newsletters from brands. I scan down and see if anything catches my eye. If it does, I open it. If not, I archive. Finally, I open my primary tab. This is 90 percent customer correspondence or business requests. I tackle this tab mostly in the order received and address each email immediately if possible. I have "canned responses" for questions and issues that come up frequently, and I use these to keep myself consistent and avoid having to rewrite responses to the same questions over and over again.

In all the above examples, I'm avoiding "decision fatigue" by simplifying some daily actions.

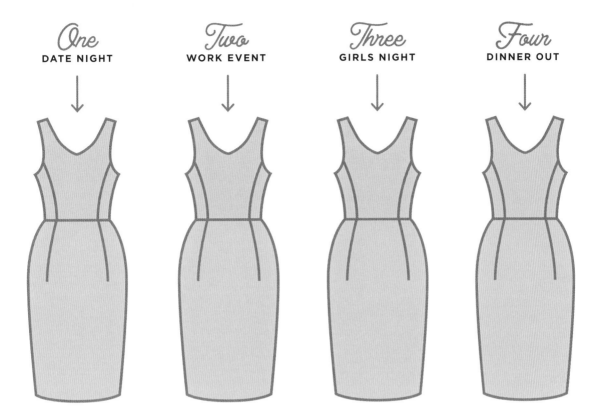

One
DATE NIGHT

Two
WORK EVENT

Three
GIRLS NIGHT

Four
DINNER OUT

I would rather spend my time on creative and challenging work projects than the routine work tasks. I would rather enjoy the anticipation of the fun night out instead of debating "the best" thing to wear to the event.

You might think this sounds horrible and boring, and if so, I hear you and respect that. I absolutely understand the joy that comes from putting together a different outfit for each event or the excitement of experimenting with your photography. I am not a complete robot and I have other areas in my life and work where trying new things and exploring options is the point.

But while my examples may not work for you, surely there are some things in your life that you can put on autopilot in order to gain more time for experimentation in your creative tasks. Maybe it's having set meals for days of the week (Meatball Monday, Taco Tuesday, and so on). Maybe it's subscribing to a service that delivers the same household consumer goods once a month. There are areas where you can simplify by taking your energy out of the decision process. Trust yourself here. Stop reinventing the wheel on routine tasks so that you can make way for more creativity in other areas.

Getting started

DETERMINING WHAT NEEDS TO BE DONE and getting your list on paper can be difficult, but sometimes knowing where to start on that list can be just as hard. There is no "wrong" way to start, but it can be paralyzing just the same.

Here are a few "getting-started" methods to consider:

THINK ABOUT YOUR PRIORITIES: What is the most important thing for you to do today? Can you do that first so it's out of the way?

BEGIN WITH THE EASY STUFF: Tasks that take just a few minutes (sending a reminder email for example) or tasks that don't take much mental energy (throwing a load of laundry into the washing machine) are good because they're simple to accomplish and can help build some momentum.

USE YOUR PEAK ENERGY ON BIG STUFF: When do you feel most alert? Don't waste those hours on email or simple task work! If you tend to have energy early in the day, use that time for your bigger projects that will involve more critical or creative thinking. If you get a rush of energy around 8 p.m. (good for you!) save those more intense projects for the evening.

GIVE YOURSELF A DEADLINE: It can be hard to stay on track throughout the day if the first project you begin takes much longer than you anticipated. Before starting a longer task, tell yourself you're going to do it for an hour (or whatever timeframe makes sense). If you're not done, you're going to move on to something else and come back to it later. Setting a time to stop ensures that you're making progress and also gives you an opportunity to check in on the project. How much time is this going to take? Can you complete it? Do you need help?

START SOMEWHERE: This may seem obvious but it's not. When you don't know where to begin, you may end up doing nothing. I urge you to push past that and find *one thing* on your list that you can do. Maybe it's easy. Maybe it will be quick. Maybe it just looks fun (or the least terrible). Begin with that, and hopefully when you return to your list you'll be able to keep moving.

Set a timer

THERE ARE SOME REOCCURRING activities in your days that just need to be cranked out. They may be never-ending tasks (like pulling weeds in the garden or sorting through paperwork), or they may be those things you don't enjoy but are mindless (like cleaning the bathroom or organizing a workspace) that you lack motivation to tackle.

Try this trick for the stuff that feels like it takes longer than it actually does or the stuff on your list you dread doing: Turn on some music or a podcast, set a timer, then GO! How much can you get done in ten minutes when you are singularly focused? How much can you get through in twenty minutes? When I do this in my kitchen, I set a timer for ten minutes and find myself whirling around, scrubbing plates, wiping down counters, and sweeping the floor with renewed energy as I try to "beat" the timer. This task I hate is only going to last ten minutes, and I am going to make those ten minutes count.

The value of white space

I MENTIONED THIS AT THE BEGINNING of this section but it's worth repeating: The point of planning is not so you have something to do every minute of every day. The point of planning is so that you *don't* have something to do every minute of every day. If you are aware of how much time you have and are aware of what has to be done, you can organize your tasks to fit within that time frame. (And if they don't all fit, you need to drop some tasks, push back your completion date, or get some help.)

Ideally, you can build in some extra space, too. Think of this as the margin of the page. It's the space where you can make additions, jot notes, and rest your eyes. It's white space— designed to be empty.

I work with a design house called Jolby and Friends to create many of the Get To Work Book products. When I first spoke with them about collaborating, they explained that J&F works to stay 80 percent booked. In other words, they take on enough projects to use 80 percent of their working hours, leaving them with 20 percent for free time. They have given themselves a healthy margin for creative exploration, passion projects, or new clients that come out of nowhere with the perfect collaboration idea. They have extra space in their business so there is room to experiment.

White space isn't just valuable in your schedule; it can be physically important, too. When I launched Get To Work Book, I planned to ship orders from my garage. The first summer, I got four pallets of planners delivered to my house and stood in the driveway with butterflies in my stomach as I unpacked that first box. Over the next year, I packed and shipped six thousand planners from my doorstep. By the spring of my second year, I realized I could no longer make this business work from my house. I had folded boxes stacked to the ceiling on my kitchen table. I had product stuffed into closets. I had no room to even think about growing the business, much less the physical space for the new product that expansion would bring.

Shortly after that realization, I went on Craigslist and began searching for a warehouse. A few weeks later, when I got the keys to a new literal white space, I felt relief. Moving the business out of my house was a risk and an expense. It was also a kick start and exactly what I needed at that time. Looking around the empty warehouse that first day, I had an idea for a new notepad I wanted to bring to the brand, and I knew I would have the space to store it once it had been printed. In my garage, my business was stifled. In this new white space, there was room to grow.

So how do you build in white space?

THE CONCEPT OF WHITE SPACE sounds great, but how do you get some? How can you actually add this margin and room in your schedule and life?

First, it's important to acknowledge that white space isn't always possible. There are seasons of work and life that are too full already, and that's okay. *That's normal.* There are periods of life where sustaining any sort of routine—much less "extra"—feels impossible (new baby, loss of a family member, illness, job change). Give yourself grace in these periods.

The second thing to recognize is that white space doesn't fall from the sky. No one is handed an extra few hours (or the keys to a warehouse) for free. It can take time, capital, and luck to get to a place where those options make sense. And while you wait, you may need to piece it together or pay for it in different ways.

Here are some smaller things you can do now to start building in white space:

DON'T REPLACE RIGHT AWAY: When a project ends or you complete a commitment, don't rush to fill the void with something else.

The same goes for stuff; if you donate ten items of clothing from your closet, don't hurry to get new shirts to hang in their place. Live with the extra time and empty hangers. See if you like this space in your schedule and closet before bringing new things into your life.

REMEMBER THAT "NOTHING" IS STILL A THING: Sometimes when I'm asked, "What are you doing next weekend?" I'll respond, "Nothing," and that's interpreted as "I'm free." There is a misconception that if "nothing" is on the agenda, then surely there is room for "something," but that's not true. "Doing nothing" is an activity. It's freedom from my schedule that gives me a chance to read or walk or nap or spend extra time making pancakes or cleaning the baseboards or all the little projects that pop up when I give myself time to sit still and get a little bored. Don't shy away from "nothing." Claim "nothing" as the something it is.

BE PROACTIVE IN SCHEDULING WHITE SPACE: How you are able to schedule in

extra time varies so much based on what season of life you are in. For some people this is as easy as putting a three-hour block each week on their shared work calendar. For others this means getting up an extra fifteen minutes early to do a yoga exercise and praying that their kids keep sleeping. Still for others it means hiring a sitter one afternoon a week to catch up on email or trading off with their partner for one evening alone at a coffee shop to write.

As you adjust in these small ways, acknowledge that *what you have is what you have*. It might feel like a postage-stamp's worth of white space, or you might have a never-ending canvas stretching out in front of you. Both of these are likely to cause panic (sometimes too much white space can hinder our creativity!), but don't let them. What you have right now is good enough to get started. Get in that extra space and take a deep breath.

Try this
Practice the one-touch rule

THE ONE-TOUCH RULE has helped me procrastinate less and prevents tasks from piling up. My goal is to touch something just once and make a decision in the moment for what to do with it. I want new things that come into my house or brain to not take up more space than needed.

I do this for email (open it, read it, respond to it, archive it), but I do it for physical things, too. When I bring in the mail I sort it into two piles: recycle and "deal with it." Into the recycle pile go bulk mailers, flyers, ads, and all the emptied envelopes from the "deal with it" pile. Then that pile goes to the recycling bin, and I put the "deal with it" on my desk. If there is time, I'll go further and pay the bill, file the form, deposit the check, or respond to my pen pal. If there is not time (like when the girls have just come home from school), I will stick the whole pile on my keyboard so it's the first thing I see the next time I am at my desk.

The idea is that I want to handle the same thing as few times as possible. I want to bring in the groceries and stick them in the pantry or fridge right away. I want to take the laundry out of the dryer and get it folded and then get those folded piles into the drawers. I want to take the order that just arrived out of the box, break the box down, and store or put the new item to use right away.

The one-touch rule prevents clutter (online and off) from piling up into something unmanageable. It helps you build a routine around staying on top of things. In the moment, it takes longer to address the item than to add it to the pile, but it's a long-term time saver and an important way to create space in your routine and home.

You're in charge; not the computer

THE BIGGEST SHIFT in my daily schedule and life came a few years ago when I stopped checking my email on my phone. I quit after I realized that so often I would need to be at my desk to properly respond to whatever had just come into my inbox. Inevitably there would be a file I needed to attach or a tracking number I had to look up, or I just wanted a full keyboard to draft a complete response. As a result, my email-checking cycle looked like this: check email on my phone, see an email that needs a response from the computer, not be able to get to my computer for a half hour, spend that entire half hour with the response email I need to draft in the back of my mind, get to computer, send response email, get away from computer, check email on my phone twenty minutes later, repeat the cycle.

It was a waste of time and mental energy and *it was completely avoidable*. I could cut out the middleman (my phone) and just check my email at my desktop a few times a day and call it done. This system has worked wonders for me. I have cut down on my active email time and decreased my stress, but my response time has not suffered in a noticeable way. Win-win.

I have also turned off most "alerts" on my phone as well. All alerts, whether they are Facebook notifications from people you hardly know or texts from your grandma, are distractions from what you're currently doing. They are your phone or device saying, "Hi, hello, look at me, I might have something more interesting to show you right now." Whatever the alert is about is almost always less important or less interesting than what you are doing, but now that you're holding the phone and it's open you might as well check your email and then scroll through Instagram and, *Oooh, she posted a new story and oh yes, I meant to look up that one thing and . . .*

These distractions take you out of whatever you're doing, and this is avoidable. You don't have to be alerted immediately. You don't have to respond immediately. You don't have to occupy a real life and an online life at the same time all the time.

The answer here isn't to give up email or give up social media (though both are possible and if you want to, I say go for it). But you must recognize that your device and the internet want 100 percent of your time. They will *always* have something for you to look at. You have to decide for yourself *when* and *how* and *where* you want to check in. Don't give that decision-making power away to your device or to "people on the internet." That power is yours. You are in charge of your actions, not the six apps that want to ding at you.

You don't have to occupy a real life and an online life at the same time all the time.

Being real about your social media use

IT'S TOUGH TO MENTION internet distractions without touching on social media in general. This is a big topic, with many books dedicated to it already, but I can't write about making time in this era without saying something about the never-ending time taker: social media.

It seems as if every few weeks I see an article, study, or statistic about how we are spending too much time on our phones and it's making us depressed and stressed. We are now less social! We are forgetting how to interact! We are holding up really high bars that can't be met! Photoshop! FOMO! This is the end of days!

Nothing about the stories surprises me. I do spend too much time on my phone (didn't need a news alert on my phone to tell me that). I do find it much easier to text someone than call them (often when my phone rings I want to throw it at the wall). I do default to mindless scrolling, and I see how easily my young kids can navigate a tablet. It does feel as though we have turned a corner as a society and it might not be for the best.

But the articles themselves are not what is important. Our reaction to these articles is what matters. The "solution" isn't to share these new statistics and moan about them. It's not to justify your time on social media. ("I need to spend time on social media for my job" is a common phrase,

but unless your job title is "social media manager," you have many other things that you also have to do for your job.) It's not to delete all your profiles and buy a cabin off the grid. No. The solution is to think about your own interaction with social media and make some choices. Do you enjoy it? Do you scroll to procrastinate? Do you scroll without thinking about it? Do you feel encouraged after scrolling? Sad after scrolling? Is this activity filling you up or is it emptying you out?

Some aspects of social media are great. Online communities have the power to generate social change, shine light on underreported issues, support small business growth, and give people who feel isolated an opportunity to say, "You feel this way, too? I am no longer alone." *This is important and valuable.*

But at the same time, social media is a lot like reality TV. It's entertaining for sure. It's also cheap to produce and it's cheap to consume. We know what to expect every time we turn it on or log in. It simultaneously feels as if we can't miss it but also if we did miss it, we wouldn't even notice. On a rare occasion what we see is excellent and fundamentally changes who we are. But 99 percent of the time it's just something to watch, and we tune in because it's on. (I say this as a person who has built a business through a social media platform and has not appeared on—but definitely auditioned for—a reality TV show.*)

Here is the worst part though: We have gotten used to this! We are so familiar with watching the minutia of other people's days and fabricated drama that we have forgotten how much other entertainment is out there. The stuff of other people's lives is now wrapped up in the stuff of our own lives, which should have so much value outside of this scrolling and watching and clicking through the #linkinprofile.

Social media is very likely here to stay. You can invite it to be a part of your media diet but it can't be all of it. If you are spending 1.4 hours a day scrolling and it makes you feel good, that's great, but hopefully you find time to consume other types of media, too. Read a book that someone wrote and someone else edited. Watch a TV show or movie that someone dreamed up and worked on for years to produce. Read a news article that was thoughtfully reported and fact-checked. Listen to music that makes you feel something powerful or a well-produced podcast about someone's experience that is vastly different from yours. Go to a museum and take in art that wasn't optimized for the latest algorithm.

"But wait!" you might say. "I don't have time to read those books or watch those shows or listen to those amazing artists." And then I would say, "You're good then! If you don't have time for 'other media,' you definitely are not spending any time on social media. You could have skipped this whole section."

Don't waste energy fretting about your social media consumption, just acknowledge it and decide if you want to cut back in order to make room for other types of media, entertainment, and—yes—joy. I have found that the more I read talented and thoughtful writers and the more I listen to or watch incredible people create, the more I am inspired in my own work. But I have to make a choice multiple times a day to not pick up my phone. I had to completely cut out Twitter in order to read the actual news as opposed to reading "hot takes" on current events. *I know that my default is going to be to scroll, so I have to actively seek out alternatives*. I don't stress about this, I just stay vigilant.

It was called Making It, hosted by Amy Poehler and Nick Offerman. It would have been my dream to get on set, but after I recorded one enthusiastic audition video, sent more than forty-two photos of finished craft projects, and then truly bombed one Skype interview, they stopped returning my emails. It's been two years. I think they went in a different direction.

Saying "yes" to the <u>right</u> things

THERE IS A MOTIVATING PHRASE that I think about a lot: *It's either "Hell yeah!" or "No."* This technique for deciding what you are going to do was developed by TED (Technology, Entertainment, Design) speaker Derek Sivers. I read of it first in the book *Essentialism* by Greg McKeown and practically shouted, "Hell yeah!" in agreement. When you practice this technique, everything feels easier (saying no can still be incredibly tough—but it *feels* easier because you have a real answer to the question of whether you should be adding something new to your plate).

What if you only said "yes!" to the tasks, projects, and ideas that you really wanted to do and said no to everything else? It would be amazing. And also impossible. Sometimes we all have to do things we don't want to out of necessity, obligation, or even guilt. It's part of being an adult human and a functioning member of society.

But there are other instances when you have a real choice over what you add to your schedule. I urge you to answer this question honestly about any project or task that crosses your plate: Is this an enthusiastic 'Absolutely yes!'? If it is, say yes. And if not, say no and move on guilt-free.

I could throw in a few hundred clichés here about how "Life is too short" and "You can't please everyone" and "YOLO," but the reality is, if you're not actually into something and don't want to do it, you're not going to do it well. You're going to procrastinate, dread it, and ultimately not show up in the way you need to for this additional task. That's unfortunate for you and everyone involved.

But when you commit to an absolute yes? When you make the decision to show up fully for something? There is nothing more exciting and rewarding. The opportunity to dig into the project you *want* to work on, the joy of expanding on that idea you can't keep down—*this is why we are here*.

We don't say "No, thanks" to be irritable, we say "No, thanks" in order to grow and expand into someone who is doing more of what they want to do. We are responding positively to what motivates us. We are signing up for the stuff that we want to do well and complete fully so we can move on to the next resounding yes.

No, no, no, no, no,
no, no, no, no, no!
YES
YES
NO,
NO
NO, NO, NO
YES,
YES,
YES!
Yes!
NO

How to find your "Absolutely yes!" tasks

THERE ARE A FEW WAYS to determine what deserves an "Absolutely yes!" response.

Listen to your gut. You already know what you want. When that email comes in or that coworker comes up to you after a meeting or that friend shoots you a text, you have an immediate reaction to their request. The question is whether you listen to that voice or if you "give it some time to think things over."

I would argue that anything you need to "think over" for too long is something you should probably say no to. That might sound horrible. How could I encourage you to rush into (or away from) such big decisions? I get it. It's scary. But big decisions are terrifying no matter how long it takes to figure out what to do. Waiting on a decision rarely makes it less scary; it just allows more time for doubt, fear, and guilt to take over.

It's easy to think the answer lies outside your own gut. You need to contact your five best friends for their insight. You need to conduct a twenty-four-hour Instagram poll. You need to reach out to your parents, your advisors, and your favorite grocery store cashier real quick.

Except: You don't. You really don't. We ask the people around us for their opinions as a way to feel things out for ourselves. We often need to say things out loud to hear how they sound. We need to be told, "YES! Go for it!" to reaffirm that we want to make this happen. Or we need to hear, "Hmmm, I don't think you should do this," to realize that in fact, *Yep, I am actually 100 percent in.*

Plus, *no one really knows what's right for you*, and so often the opinions of your five friends, your Instagram followers, your parents, and the grocery cashier are not going to line up. Suddenly you've taken this choice—this choice that belongs to you—and you've opened it up to the concerns, insecurities, and baggage of a crowd. Yikes. Now that is actually terrifying.

You can learn from past mistakes. Gut feeling or not, you have to make decisions. One thing that helps me separate the "YES!" from the "No, thanks" is to think back on similar things I have done. I have committed to projects that were not right. I have signed up for events I dreaded doing. I have turned in poor results because I had no interest in the work. All of that is sad and it's often painful to recall. But I have to remember those times in order to not make the same mistakes again.

When I commit to things that were not "Absolutely yes!" I always hit a point where I wonder, "Why did I sign up for this?" and in those moments I remind myself that it's too late now. I need to finish the best I can, but *next time*? Next time I have an opportunity to say no.

You will make mistakes. You get to make mistakes. But you don't have to keep making the same mistakes.

Sleep on it. If you can't clearly hear your gut and you have no prior example to compare this decision to, sleep on it. Are you tossing and turning over doing the thing? Are you tossing and turning over not doing the thing? There's your answer. *Go with the choice that will allow you to fall asleep faster tomorrow night.*

And if you go to bed with this decision on your mind and fall right to sleep without a single thought? Great news! This is clearly not that big of a deal. Do it! Or don't! There is a good chance it won't matter much a week from now.

You will make mistakes.
You get to make mistakes. But you don't have to keep making the same mistakes.

Try this

Step back from
your phone

IF YOU DO FEEL LIKE YOU SPEND TOO MUCH TIME scrolling or you just want to experiment with less social media time, I have a few simple suggestions for things you can try today:

- **Wear a (nonsmart) watch and get a real clock.** Don't let your phone be the only "time teller" in your life. Don't give yourself one more reason to pick it up.

- **Use your phone to help monitor your screentime.** You can take advantage of new setting features or download an app that tracks your phone usage. For a few days, see how many minutes you spend scrolling. Then try to cut that down. Can you spend fifteen fewer minutes a day? How about twenty? Shoot for something achievable.

- **Delete the apps that suck most of your time.** Years ago this meant taking the mail app off my home screen. More recently it meant deleting Twitter. I don't use Facebook, but I know some folks who have taken it off their phones. I have gone weekends without Instagram. It's shocking how often I still pick up the phone mindlessly to scroll these apps, but when the apps are not there, I can't. (This is often my reminder to pick up something other than my phone.)

- **Pick a time where you'll "catch up" on social media** and give yourself a limit to how long you'll scroll. Remember, there is always going to be something there that's begging for our attention. Our brains are now conditioned to expect that dopamine hit from "something new!" You have to limit this the way you'd limit any potentially addictive substance.

- **Give yourself literal space!** Keep your phone in the trunk of your car when you're driving. Keep the phone out of your bedroom. Designate a top shelf in your kitchen where the phone sits between 5 and 8 p.m. while you're cooking dinner and spending time with your partner or kids. Experiment and see what might work for you and how you feel about that distance between your fingers and your phone.

Respecting the ebb and flow

SOMETHING I CAN PROMISE is that in your daily work and schedule you will have moments when everything is working perfectly and moments when you can't catch a break. When things are flowing, you'll feel unstoppable, and when it's all crumbling around you, you'll panic.

Our highest highs and lowest lows are memorable because they are extreme. They feel big and important but they are also rare (this is what makes them so intense in hindsight). The bulk of life happens in the moments that exist inside the "normal" (or the times between the major ebbs and flows of energy).

Remember this cycle exists, and respect it. You will run out of patience and ideas and your energy will wane. In these moments, relax. Give yourself time to slow down. Step away from your sewing project, IKEA cabinet construction, or book proposal, and take a break. Trust that the ideas will return and you'll find your way back to normal. (Try the "three things" exercise on page 43!) There will be other days when you are bursting with energy and creativity and your hands can't keep up with how fast your brain is generating thoughts. This, too, is temporary. You will return to normal again, and that's okay.

Years ago I realized that if I made decisions on my most productive days, I would be overworked, overwhelmed, and in debt with one hundred employees. And if I made decisions on my worst days, I would be underworked, underwhelmed, and would live alone in a mountaintop cabin.

In both cases, I would lose in a big way. I would be taking a temporary situation and trying to build something permanent on it. Normal ebbs and flows of your balance and creativity don't last (which ultimately is a good thing).

While you can't avoid either, you can be prepared for both. When I am feeling overly excited and motivated, I have a list of projects to tackle, and suddenly, they all feel doable. When I am feeling down, a mantra I like to return to is "You have had good ideas before and you'll have good ideas again." It's true! And it reminds me that the only thing I can do is keep showing up. Some days I am ready to climb Mount Everest and some days the fridge feels far away. But on neither day am I "better" than the other. On all days I am just me. I'm just doing what I can for that day. That is enough. What you are bringing each day is enough; just keep bringing it.

The only thing you can control is that **you keep showing up.**

This is about you (stop comparing!)

I WENT TO A BLOGGERS' CONFERENCE years ago and the keynote speaker was Martha Stewart. After the discussion ended, she took questions from the audience. (This is a memory, so the dialogue isn't exact, but it's close.)

An audience member stood up and asked, "I don't understand how you do all of this. You have a magazine and a TV show, you're doing so many things, and you still find time to blog. I am just trying to blog and raise my kid, and I am struggling to find the time. How do you do it all?"

Martha Stewart didn't say anything for a second, and then she said, "I have a lot of help with this. There is a team of people behind the Martha Stewart brand."

There is a team of people behind the Martha Stewart brand.

In theory we all know this. We know that Martha Stewart isn't the only person working on her magazine. She isn't single-handedly doing all the crafts, taking all the photos, booking all the guests, and running around New York City for supplies. We get that there is more going on behind the scenes.

It's therefore important that you do not compare who you are and what you are doing to Martha Stewart (or any famous personality). But it's *just as important* that you don't compare yourself to *anyone*. There is always going to be "that person" who is "ahead" of you in life. Or that person who *just started* her business and already (appears!) to have double the sales. Or that neighbor who has it all together. Or that [you get the idea].

"That person" isn't going anywhere. You can decide to follow their every move and wonder how they do it all, or you can put your head down and focus on the things that you are doing. I follow and watch and cheer for a large number of people online and in real life. I am excited to see how their businesses grow. I enjoy seeing their work and life success. I believe that there is enough room for all the good ideas (and that includes mine and theirs!).

But I don't follow on social media any of my business competitors (which right now are other brands or individuals who are making day planners). This isn't because I don't like them (in

Keep your eyes on your own paper as you write your own story.

fact if we knew each other in real life, I would probably love them!), it's because I don't want to envy them. I don't want to see new work from them and fear that I am not producing something new fast enough. I don't want to see their engagement skyrocket and wonder why mine hasn't grown in the same way. *I don't want to question my worth in the space by comparing myself to how much space someone else is taking up.*

This might seem like a mistake. Shouldn't I be studying my competitors? Shouldn't I know what they are doing? Shouldn't I be learning from them and challenging myself by pushing my brand alongside theirs?

Maybe.

Except right now, my brand is me. I am not Martha Stewart with a team of people behind me. I have the energy and the enthusiasm to run this business the way I can and at this moment: with my head down. I can listen to my customers. I can listen to my mentors. I can listen to my gut. But I can't compare. I can look behind me at how far I have come. I can look in front of me at where I want to go. And I can look down at where I am at. There is no need to look side to side.

Remember, where you are is where you are. Who you are is who you are. It's okay to want more! It's okay to strive for better! But your path is not going to look like anyone else's, and so following someone else's map will only be discouraging. Keep your eyes on your own paper as you write your own story.

Get back on the horse

THERE WILL BE TIMES when your schedule will be upset. You will get sick. Your kid will get sick. The car battery will die. The flight will be canceled. Maybe you will find yourself struggling to settle into a routine when you return to work after an extended leave (or even a long weekend). Maybe you just added a new baby or puppy to your family, and it's taking much more out of you than you thought.

When you find yourself off your game and out of your routine, you have to do three things in order to get back on the horse:

COMMUNICATE: Tell the people around you (coworkers, friends, partners) what's up and why things may be delayed for a while. Don't make excuses; just explain the situation and ideally reschedule for a realistic date or time that you can meet your missed deadline. If there is a specific way that they can help you get back on track, *ask for it*.

FOCUS ON WHAT YOU CAN DO: Is there anything small that you can get done while the big things are on hold? Remember the three things exercise (page 43)? Little things are still important and progress in any area is still progress.

GIVE YOURSELF GRACE: This thing that you are going through is new. You don't have to power through this. You can take your time to heal or help or adjust. You have an out-of-your-control reason to slow down—take it. Everything will be here when you get back. There is no rush.

You have enough time

WE HAVE ALL HAD THAT FEELING that there is just not enough time. I used to joke to my husband that I wished I could "press pause" on the world for a few hours. I loved the idea that everyone else would have to be still while I got to rush around catching up on all the things. (Basically I was wishing for a Time-Turner from the Harry Potter books.) Unfortunately, that technology is not here yet, and I am not a wizard, so thankfully, I have found a more practical way to look at my time.

I believe that we have exactly enough time for all the things that matter to us.

Let me tell you about the project that helped me to realize this.

For the past decade, I have participated in an annual challenge that my friend Ali Edwards calls One Little Word. The concept is simple: you choose a "guiding word" for the year that you want to focus on or invite into your life. I see it as an opportunity to set an overall intention, and I usually come up with some goals in various areas of my life that connect with the word.

In 2016 I chose the word *enough*. The year before had been one of growth; I had launched Get To Work Book and our second daughter, Piper, had joined our family. As I entered the new year, I felt overstretched. I had a two-year-old in part-time childcare and a two-month-old who was at home with me all day. I had a new business that was outgrowing my garage and a husband who was spending all of his nonworking hours studying for an exam that was essential for his career. I had enough to worry about, and I didn't want to add anything to the juggle.

In the early spring I got an email from someone who had read my blog for a few years. "What are your hobbies right now? I always loved following your quilting projects." I thought about it for a few minutes before realizing I didn't *have* any hobbies right now. I was staying afloat (which felt like a big deal), but there were no layer 3 projects on the horizon. I wasn't sure I remembered what working on layer 3 felt like.

A few weeks later I heard about The 100 Day Project, an open challenge hosted by artist Elle Luna that asks participants to spend one hundred consecutive days doing a creative project and sharing daily photos of their process on social media. Some people paint, some doodle, some cook meals, some write poems. Some focus narrowly on one subject and explore it deeply. Others cast a wide net and take on something broad.

I was intrigued but conflicted. Old Elise (the girl with all the hobbies) would have loved this adventure. Current Elise (the girl who had enough on her plate) didn't have the space (mentally or physically) for a big craft project. I couldn't make anything with my hands; I had a baby who was still nursing around the clock and a toddler who was adjusting to being a big sister. But despite my declaration of *enough*, I wanted to go for it anyway. I needed some sort of jump start. What was the worst thing that could happen? I wouldn't be able to do it? I was okay with that.

I decided to share one hundred pep talks. I was going to write a pep talk to myself and share it with the internet via Instagram caption every day for one hundred days. I had no idea if this project would be easy or hard (one hundred days is difficult to conceptualize until you're in it), but dang, I needed a hobby, and this would take place on my phone, so it wasn't going to add to the mess in my house.

It's not an exaggeration to say that this project changed my life. It wasn't the pep talks them-selves, it was the experience of writing them. It was committing to something daily and choosing to follow through. I wrote thirteen thousand words in the Notes app of my phone during the free pockets of my day. I wrote in line at the gro-cery store, on an airplane, while nursing Piper, while sitting in my car before preschool pickup. I dictated pep talks while pushing the stroller. I typed while brushing my teeth. I found the time to jot something down and push "Share" for one hundred days in a row.

And something special happened as I did this. The more pockets I found for writing, the more pockets I found for other things. I started sewing again during those one hundred days. I signed up for a pottery class at a local studio halfway through the challenge. In order to find perspective and have something to write about, I had to spend less time online and more time on life. I started telling myself that I had enough time, and through this attitude change, I found that I did.

You have enough time. You have enough time. You have enough time. I would type this over and over again if I thought it would make you believe it, but it won't. *You* have to say it. You have to write it on a sticky note and attach it to your mirror. You have to pick something extra—some project or hobby you have been meaning to return to or something brand-new to explore—and you have to decide it's important to you and worth carrying in your pockets.

"It's not that easy though, because I have [insert thing here]." I hear you. I do. I didn't say it was "easy." This is about telling yourself an entirely different story than the one you've been hearing for years. We don't say "I have enough time" because it's magic and it will conjure up time or clear our schedule. We say "I have enough time" because "I am too busy for _____" is a solid argument that needs to be countered. If you say you're too busy, you'll believe it. If you're "too busy to read," you will never pick up the book. If you're "too busy to spend time with friends," you'll never say yes to the invitation to grab coffee. If you're "too busy to do that one thing," you'll never have time to do that one thing.

So what if, just for a week, you stopped saying it? What if instead you said, "I have exactly enough time for _____." What would happen? What would you put into that blank space? ➥

You have exactly enough time for the things that matter to you.

Part 3

Let's Dream Bigger

Wherever you are on your journey, progress is possible.

Where to <u>start?</u>

FOR SOME PEOPLE, this section of the book, where I encourage you to start dreaming bigger, is going to be much more intimidating than the last part, where I asked you to think about making space in your schedule. Clearing space, even when it's hard, is task work. *Do this one thing more efficiently or cut out this one unnecessary thing and ta-da! Space!* But "dreaming bigger" is more abstract. It can feel overwhelming. Maybe when you think about "dreaming big," your brain explodes with possibility. Or maybe it's been so long since you let yourself "dream" that you have no place to start.

It's possible that you picked up this book with an objective in mind already. You might have a business you want to launch or a job you'd love to get. Or maybe you're excited to add a new hobby to your life or learn something new. You might already be halfway to realizing your big dream. Or maybe you're still far from the starting line. All these things are okay. Wherever you are on your "dreaming big" journey, progress is possible.

This section is about adding to your life. It's where we will explore the layer 3 tasks—the stuff that you do because you *want* to. These are the extras that may feel impossible at first but make a big difference in your attitude and quality of life (basically, they are the guacamole to your taco).

Do you know what you want more of? Can you picture the bonus stuff you'd choose to add?

In this section we will explore how to take something abstract (an idea or goal) and turn it into something concrete that you can describe, talk about, and break into actionable steps. Dreams are great! But to make progress, they have to become something solid.

What's a <u>goal,</u> anyway?

IN THE BEGINNING OF THE BOOK I shared what makes a goal "good," but I want to give some concrete examples of goals I have set and worked toward over the past decade. I've broken them down in categories to share how varied they have been.

Business:

Since 2011 I have set a financial goal for how much money I want my business to net (total profit minus total expenses) for the year. In the beginning, this was so I could justify not having a job outside of "working for myself." I wanted to make $30,000 to match my salary at my previous retail job. Nine years later, I still set this goal at the beginning of each year to have an idea how much I'll contribute to my household and so I can accurately pay estimated income taxes.

This annual number helps me think through all business ventures and expenses. It also works as a motivator. In October 2017, I was falling short of my financial goal for the year and knew I couldn't get there without doing something extra. I launched an e-course called Encouraging Creative Kids. An e-course is time intensive to create (I put in about one hundred hours), but it has low overhead (I didn't have to spend money to make it happen). Committing to a big project like this got me over the finish line for my annual goal.

When I turned twenty-nine, I launched a business venture called MAKE29. It was a year-long project where I committed to selling a unique product in limited editions of 29 or 290 each month for a year. My objective was to make money, but also to explore some new crafts and determine what direction I wanted to take my business. This framework was clearly expressed at the outset (one project per month) and my challenge was to fill in the frame each month with a new product.

Fitness:

I have had various fitness goals over the years—be able to do the splits (still hasn't happened), run a half marathon (finished two), attend 120 Pilates classes in a year (as I edit this, I'm still on track).

I have also had more "daily-challenge"–focused goals. For years I wore a step tracker and committed to taking ten thousand steps a day. I also participated for three years in a challenge called "Mile a Day" where the goal is to run a mile every day from Thanksgiving to New Year's.

I have set goals around food. After reading *Animal, Vegetable, Miracle* in 2012, I ate only locally grown veggies and fruits for a summer (we were living in Central California at the time, and this was hardly a challenge). I tried the Whole30 diet in 2015 (it wasn't a good fit for me). In the next few years, I would love to grow more of our own veggies and eat just from our yard for a month. (Right now that seems impossible but inspiring.)

Creative:

My first big creative challenge was in 2007, when I decided to decorate a playing card every day for a year. The cards worked as a mini canvas and journal, and I painted, collaged, stamped, and sewed them. I didn't finish this challenge (I stopped right around card 270), but in so many ways this daily art project started my goal-setting career.

When I turned twenty-six I set a goal to complete twenty-six craft projects. Throughout the year I made a variety of things. I sewed a dress, painted a canvas, made a wreath out of driftwood, and on and on. This was one of the first big projects that I finished on time and with energy.

For the past few years, I have participated in The 100 Day Project I mentioned in part 2. In 2016, I shared "100 Pep Talks." In 2017, I attempted "100 Plants on Fabric" and created a quilt from one hundred varied fabric squares. In 2018 I worked toward "100 Craft Adventures" and committed to the broad goal of doing something creative for at least fifteen minutes each day.

Lifestyle:

In 2011 I set a goal to bake forty different loaves of bread. I chose this goal because baking bread was intimidating to me, and I figured a good way to get over it was to get into it. It took longer than the year to finish, but I did complete the challenge.

For a few years in my early twenties, I set birthday goals lists. The first year I made a list of twenty-three things I wanted to do while twenty-three. The goals on these lists ranged from "take a ten-mile hike" to "enter a contest" to "print more photos" to "plan a date night each month." The goals on the list were all over the map and (as start-of-a-new-year goals tend to be) ambitious! I rarely accomplished more than half the list each year, but I loved having a focus and something to refer to when I "needed something to do."

As I'm writing this in 2018, I am on a no-clothes-buying challenge and have committed to buying no shoes, accessories, or clothing for myself. I have two choices if I want something new: go without or make it.

These are a small fraction of the challenges I have set and worked toward, and while they vary in scope and difficulty, they have similarities. Most have a clear time period and were set around a significant event (a new calendar year or my birthday). Some are part of public challenges or are things that I saw someone do and thought might be something I would connect well with. All are things that were easy to document and I was willing to state out loud either to the internet or to friends and family.

I use goal-setting as a way to break the mundane and the routine in my days. I love having something to work toward and to do outside of the "normal." These sorts of challenges give me that.

I also often have more than one thing going at a time. Right now, as I write this, I am about 75 percent through my third hundred-day project. I am trying to get in 120 Pilates classes. I am well aware of my business financial goal and can tell you within a few hundreds of dollars how close I am to reaching it. Like everything else, I have added my goals in layers so they are no longer a source of overwhelm, but of joy.

What to do when you have too many ideas

YOU MAY FIND THAT when you think about goals you want to be working on, too many ideas come to mind. I actually hear most frequently from people who suffer from this holdup. It sounds like a good problem, but having too many ideas can bury you to the point where it's impossible to know where to begin. It's overwhelming to pick one thing to start. So many "too many ideas" folks never seem to be able to get moving. If this is you, I've got an exercise for you to try.

You'll need a pen and a notebook or notepad. You'll also need a timer (your phone will work, but turn it on airplane mode—no distractions).

Ready? Okay.

Go through the notebook and write one idea at the top of each page. Every single idea you have that's crowding your brain, get it out of your head and onto its own sheet of paper. Don't edit or think them through, just write them down. You might have five. You might have five hundred. That's okay. Keep going until you're out of ideas.

Now, let's expand on those ideas.

Get your timer ready. Give yourself five minutes per page to dive into each idea. Write down every extra thought you have that's associated with each idea. What would it take to bring this to life? What excites you about this? What would you call it? Who can help you? What's the color scheme? What do you need to get started? What would be your first step? Use your five minutes to give each idea as detailed a framework as possible. Build them out on paper.

Do this for every idea you have until you're done.

Something interesting should have happened here. You most likely lost a little steam as you flipped through the notebook. You may have noticed that you didn't really have extra thoughts on ideas 7 through 13. (You may have actually noticed you didn't even have ideas 7 through 13.) That's okay. *That's actually great.*

Hopefully you also picked up on something else . . . that there was one idea, one page in your notebook, where you couldn't write fast enough. Those five minutes flew by and you could have kept going and going for an hour. Good news—*that's your idea.* You may have *too many ideas*, but you also have *one idea* that's ready to roll. This idea is your starting point. This idea is what you need to be working on right now.

Take your notebook, and stick it in a special place. It's yours, and those ideas belong to you. Let them go for now. You have found your focus, and it's time to get to work on your *one* idea.

It's time to get to work on your one idea.

What to do when you have <u>no</u> ideas

SO WHAT IF YOU HAVE the opposite problem? What if you don't know what you want to be doing right now? How can you tackle this?

There are a few ways.

First, it can be helpful to think back on a period in your life when you were doing something you loved. Maybe it was when you were a kid. Or a class you took in high school. Or something you did before you had kids. Or before you started that big job. What were the activities that you enjoyed doing "back when you had time"?

Second, determine one area that you'd like to improve on. Maybe you want to be more flexible. Or maybe you would like to be a better sketch artist, or you want to stay in touch with friends, or know more about current events. What is one thing you think might be missing?

Third, look forward into the future. How do you want to be spending your time? What would you like your days to look like in five years? In ten years? Maybe you want to run an ultramarathon. Great! Today would be a good day to start training for a 5K. *Having an idea of where you want to be headed can help you decide what you need to be doing now.*

All these questions are just jump starts. Their objective is to help you capture a feeling and figure out a desire. What did you enjoy? What would you like to know? Where do you want to be going?

It's important to remember that this is just a starting point. The thing you try first doesn't have to be a permanent change. If one idea doesn't work out, you'll have another one. Something else will come along. But you can't sit and wait for that idea to strike or fall into your lap. The "next great idea" will come because you have been actively trying all the good ideas before it.

Once you've asked the questions, answer them. From these answers you can get closer to coming up with what you want to work on.

Try this
Develop a
five-year plan

I SAY *FIVE-YEAR PLAN* and I see people panic a bit. *What is this? A business? Do I need a spreadsheet? I don't know what I want for dinner tonight; please don't make me think about five years in the future.*

I hear you. But stay with me for a second.

A five-year plan is an opportunity to think boldly and creatively about your own life. I recommend a five-year timeline because it's far enough off to make you feel like anything is possible but also soon enough that this doesn't feel like a complete fantasy. Remember, you're not locking yourself into anything. When done correctly, completing this exercise has little to do with five years from now and everything to do with today.

To make your five-year plan you'll need a pen, a pencil, and a piece of paper. Determine three or four areas that you'd like to consider. A few suggestions: family, living situation, work, self, physical health, mental health, education, faith. Divide your paper into three or four sections and label them with your chosen categories with your pen.

Before you dive into the unknown, write down the known. How old will you be in five years? What about your kids? Do you know what level you might be at work? Anything you may potentially know about your life five years from now should be written on paper.

And then, before looking forward, take a quick glance backward. Where were you five years ago? How old were you? What were you doing? This part

is key. Often when you think back on the past five years you realize that a lot has changed! This is good news! This means a lot can change again.

Now grab your pencil and start writing. In five years, what would you like to be doing with your work? What would you like your family situation to be? Where do you want to be living? What is important for you to see and do and accomplish over the next five years?

I made my first five-year plan in the summer of 2017 when I was thirty-two. I had just finished a big creative project, and I was feeling underwhelmed and unsure of what I wanted to be doing next. I divided my paper into three areas: family/house, work, self.

Under "family/house" I wrote the mundane (fix our leaking bathroom shower), the grand (purchase a house in Tahoe), and everything in between (travel with the girls to Yellowstone, take a ten-year anniversary trip, improve our master bedroom, add cement tiles to the backyard patio).

Under "work" I wrote goals for my business: more speaking engagements, write a goal-setting book, transfer Get To Work Book shipping responsibilities, get out of my warehouse lease.

Under "self" I wrote a wide range of things from my health (make yoga a priority) to creative (learn to screen print and fill in our succulent garden) to more personal (make more local friends and build an ethical wardrobe).

5

Self

Family/House

Work

Making your five-year plan can be a deeply personal task or it can be something you do with a partner or friend. If you have older children, you could consider doing one for the whole family together. This is not something you are going to hammer into stone and hang over your fireplace; instead, this is a living document. It's a guideline and a flexible plan. You are going to change, and your wants and goals can change as you do. This plan is designed to give you some perspective and an ideal place that you're headed so that you feel motivated to act today.

Today you a
to take a sm
forward so f
from now yo
look back a
*Wow, look h
have come.*

e going
all step
ve years
u will
d think,
ow *far I*

Pick three action items

IF YOU TOOK THE TIME TO DRAFT a five-year plan, awesome. The next step is to start working toward it. This is more difficult. It's easy to think hypothetically into the future and hope for things. But to realize them, you must take action.

Look at all the areas and items on your list. Pick three of the things that you wrote down. Now pick three small things that you can do *this week* to start on the path toward those goals.

When I did this in July 2017, these were my three action items:

- **Call the contractor** for a quote to fix the shower.

- **Email the book agent** who had contacted me a few months ago.

- **Get a few more** succulent propagation containers.

That was it. Those three tiny things were all I had to do to start down the road to realizing my five-year plan. Making that phone call would take five minutes. Writing and sending that email would take maybe

ten. The succulent containers were something I could pick up on my next trip to the hardware store.

And that's the point. Your first few action items will be small. There is a misconception that "big dreams" deserve big kickoff parties, press releases, and fireworks. That's usually wrong. Big dreams begin with small action, not fanfare. Your first few steps should be so insignificant that it seems like there is no point in actually doing them. But there is . . . the five-year plan is the point. You are taking tiny action in a predetermined direction today so that you can be in a new place five years from now.

What small thing can you do today? Maybe you can search online for yoga videos or download a meditation app. Maybe today you are going to sign up for that cooking class your friend recently raved about. Maybe today you are going to bring lunch from home to save $10 for that dream vacation to Italy. Maybe today you are going to walk around the block. Maybe today you are going to buy some colored pencils and a fresh notebook.

Maybe today you are going to take a small step forward so five years from now you will look back and think, *Wow, look how far I have come.*

Big dreams begin with small action, not fanfare.

Turning dreams into concrete

THE PURPOSE OF BOTH brainstorming exercises—both for "no ideas" and for "too many ideas"—is not just to give you a place to start. It's also to take you out of the abstract. One of the reasons you may feel overwhelmed with goal-setting is because you let yourself dwell in a lot of what-ifs.

What if I tried what she is doing? What if I went back to school like he did? What if I quit my job? What if I started that business? What if I try that? What if I don't like this? What if it's too hard? What if I am wasting my time?

This wondering is good if it makes you curious and encourages you to try. This wondering is bad if you confuse it with action. It's easy to feel "busy" when your brain is crowded with thoughts. But to make progress, you need to get those thoughts on paper and turn them into something actionable. You need to sort through what actually matters and clear out the extra clutter so that you can get serious about your real ideas.

How you fe
the work th
create mat
seriously y
the things
matters.

el about
at you
ers. How
ou take
you do

Your ideas and voice are valuable; take them seriously

I MENTIONED AT THE BEGINNING of the book that for a long time I have struggled to say what I do for a living. No matter how long I have been doing this or how well things are going, I can't articulate what I do for a living correctly. It's become an awkward joke, but it's something I need to work on. I need to pick a title and own it.

It's funny—when I meet someone and they tell me they are an artist, I don't demand to see their portfolio. I don't ask someone who says they run a business to show me their books. I have yet to request to see a law school diploma from an attorney. Nope. Instead, I hear their response and believe them.

I spoke recently to a friend for my podcast and she mentioned that it was a pivotal moment in her career when she changed her online bio to say she was an artist. Prior to this she went with the (for her) less substantial term of *maker*. Switching to *artist* gave her validation. It didn't necessarily change what her customers or her friends thought about her work, but it did change how she felt about it. This is key. How you feel about the work that you create matters. How seriously you take the things you do matters.

Please note: This is not just about your professional work or the things you want to do to make money. Even the things that you do "just for fun" should be treated as important. Your hobbies should be given weight and value. Time to exercise or time to just sit and do nothing should be taken seriously. *Seriously* doesn't need to mean *serious*. It just means important, valuable, and of substance. When you begin to take the things that you are doing or want to be doing seriously, you allow those activities to have their significant space. You are saying, "Yes. This thing is meaningful and I am adding it to my life because it is important to me."

That is what this is about. Part of how you give yourself the space for your dreams is making sure that *you* know they matter. The world doesn't have to take them seriously. The world doesn't have to think what you are doing or what you want to do is important. But if you think it's important? *It is. It's important to you. Own that.*

Say your goals out loud

ONE WAY TO TAKE YOUR GOALS SERIOUSLY is to start saying them out loud.

I often have to argue my case when I recommend doing this. There is a lot of fear about saying your goals out loud. What if someone "steals" your idea? What if people tell you it can't be done? What if you fail or lose interest or quit before you finish?

I hear you and I want to address these concerns.

WHAT IF SOMEONE *TAKES* YOUR IDEA? If what you are creating is brand-new and has never been done before, then yes, treat your idea with the utmost secrecy. But surely you need to tell someone, yes? They will want to know why you are always at the lab or on the computer. Have them sign nondisclosure agreements if it helps you feel better. Most likely though, you are not going to be working on something that needs high-level security clearance. It's also likely that what *you* are bringing to this idea is what matters. Sure, someone else could attempt it, but do they have what you have? Probably not.

WHAT IF PEOPLE TELL YOU IT CAN'T BE DONE? This response can actually be helpful. For me, when someone says it's "impossible,"

I like to check in and think through my idea to come to terms with any doubts I may be feeling. *Can I do this? Do I want to do this?* If yes, I press forward despite the naysayers. And if no? Awesome—it's one less project to think about. Thank your critics for helping you to realize this was a no-go early. (Early is the best time to fail.)

WHAT IF YOU FAIL OR LOSE INTEREST OR QUIT BEFORE YOU FINISH? This is not unlikely. You will share your goals and dreams out loud and then not reach or realize them. It's common. So common, in fact, that the people whom you told will understand. It's part of the process and more than okay.

So yes, there may be some "risk" to speaking your goals out loud, but the rewards are far greater.

Often, speaking your goals (or writing them down and pushing "Publish") is the best way to confirm that you're really on board with your plan. Sometimes the fact that you can't say it out loud means you're not quite ready to commit (and that's okay!). You can put your idea on hold for now until you're ready to tell people about it.

Tabling your idea is a good thing! It means while that idea sits on the table, you can explore something else. *What can you come up with that you want to shout from the rooftops? What idea are you excited to explain to your friend? What is something that is more realistic for the place you're in right now?*

Once you share your plan, it's likely that you'll get help realizing it. When you speak your goals out loud, you give other people a chance to hear them. *Your wish, your dream, your goal now exists on someone else's radar.* That thing you are working toward? It just became one step closer to reality. And remember, the objective here is to take the unreal—the stuff that currently feels unbelievable or unrealistic—and make it into something tangible.

You say your goals out loud so that someone else can ask, "Hey, how's that going? Did you email that agent yet? Have you talked to the gallery about hosting your work? Are you buying that plane ticket? When can I read your first draft? Do you need me to watch the kids so you can go for a run?"

You say your goals out loud so that when you start to feel doubt, someone else is in your corner and can support you. You say your goals out loud so when others doubt your idea, you can figure out how committed you really are to your plan. You say your goals out loud so that they feel possible.

A big part of this is just getting more comfortable. I worked on the concept for this book for over a year and the actual writing for about five months. I was nervous to officially tell the internet that I was starting this project, but I knew that for me, it was an important step in the process. I took a photo, wrote (and rewrote) a caption, hit "Share," and then avoided my phone.

When I finally checked in, with flushed cheeks and a knot in my stomach, I was relieved to find that the responses were overwhelmingly positive, and I was encouraged to note that it now felt real. This was a thing I was going to do now. It would either be a success or a flop or land somewhere in the middle, but it would happen and happen publicly.

I didn't "become an author" when I shared my intentions. I was technically going to become an author regardless of whether anyone knew about it, but sharing it out loud made it real. It got me fired up to start writing on Monday. Sharing my progress with my Instagram followers as I wrote kept me motivated to keep writing and editing and fixing. "I am writing a book." It's a powerful phrase. Not powerful enough to do the work for me, but powerful enough to motivate me to do the work.

Try this
Start an accountability group

YOU DON'T HAVE TO TELL a bunch of strangers what you are working on (and of course some projects will demand a bit more secrecy), but it may help to tell a small group. Consider starting an "accountability group" with friends or colleagues. Find four to six people, and commit to meeting once a month in real life or via video chat to share what you're working on.

This is the pitch you can send to whomever you want to invite:

"Hi! I believe there is power in speaking your goals out loud and having people around you to keep you on track. I would love to hear what you're working on. Would you like to join my accountability group? We will meet monthly on [insert day] for just [insert set period of time]. This is an opportunity to speak your intentions for the next month, ask for help or advice if you need it, and most important, share one thing you're going to do today to make progress. Are you in?"

And if you and I were in an accountability group together, here's what I would tell you at our meeting today: "My goal for the next month is to finish writing this book. I am decently on track but have about twelve thousand words to write. Ideally I would like to be done with the bulk of the text by mid-month so I can spend two weeks editing. If someone can shoot me an encouraging text around mid-month, that would be great. Today, when we get off this call, I am going to go for a quick walk and come home and rework a chapter that has been bugging me."

Everyone in the group can be working on different things (some people may have health goals or family goals; others may be trying to complete a work project) or your group members may be all working toward similar goals. Either way is great as long as competition is low and you are able to be honest about what you're working on, what you need, and if you are struggling.

Commit to this group. Commit to sharing honestly and keeping the meetings short and on track. Commit to being held accountable and holding the others who show up accountable. Tremendous work can come from this group.

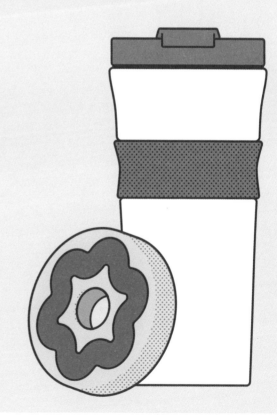

You get to be scared

RECENTLY, MY DAUGHTER Ellerie had to get a few shots at her wellness checkup. On the way home from the doctor I told her I was proud of her for being so brave. "I wasn't brave," she responded in a huff. "I was scared."

"Yes, exactly! But you did it anyway. That's bravery."

I think it went over her head, but the point extends to all ages. You are brave not because you don't feel fear. You are brave *because* you feel fear. Being brave isn't avoiding the tough situations; it's recognizing them and figuring out how to get through them.

People often use the term *fearless* to describe someone who is going for something or attempting something "scary." This is a problem. If you think someone is fearless or somehow living without fear, then you assume that you, too, should feel less or even no fear when attempting something for the first time. When you find yourself scared or uncertain, you may not be willing to push forward.

As you attempt larger goals and try new things, a normal and frequent emotion will be fear. Sometimes this will be butterflies in your stomach, and other times it will be almost crippling. Don't let this fear on its own convince you not to do something. Don't let this fear fool you into thinking you're inadequate. Don't let this fear keep you from trying. Don't try to fight it or squash it. *You get to be scared. Doing new things is scary.* The unknown brings risk, and most people are hesitant to engage with risk.

But despite your nerves, you can do it anyway. You can be scared *and* simultaneously take the leap. In her book *Big Magic*, Elizabeth Gilbert describes this as "taking your fear for a ride." She suggests inviting the fear or doubt into the backseat of the car. It gets to come along, but the point is you are still embarking on the trip. I love this idea.

Over time, as you set and meet goals and attempt different things, you might expect the fear to dissipate, but it's much more likely it will always be there. You'll just become familiar with feeling scared. You may even start to welcome the fear because you'll know it means you're about to do something big.

Something to note: I often hear from people who don't want to attempt something new

You are brave not because you don't feel fear. You are brave *because* you feel fear. Being brave isn't avoiding the tough situations; it's recognizing them and figuring out how to get through them.

Play out the
worst-case scenario

WHEN I AM FEELING TOO SCARED or overwhelmed about something that I have to do, I often will mentally play out the worst-case scenario. *What is the worst thing that can happen here?* And if the answer isn't, "Someone could die or be seriously injured," then usually the "worst case" is bearable.

For so many of the things that challenge us, the "worst case"—when turned into something concrete—is actually manageable.

You could fall down. You could embarrass yourself. You could lose money. You could fail. You could . . . what? What else is *your* worst case?

Think through these situations when you're feeling scared. What sort of precautions can you take to make them less of a big deal?

Can you wear different shoes? Can you test the floor or running track ahead of time? And what if you fall? Couldn't you just get up again?

Can you practice your speech? Can you get more information about the people or the event so you are more prepared and know what to

expect? And what if you do say something awkward? Couldn't you just apologize and move on?

Can you adjust the investment? Can you split the payment? Can you explore more pricing options? Is the potential payoff from this investment worth the risk? And what if you do lose the investment? Couldn't you resave and try something else?

Can you lower the risks? Can you do a trial run? Can you try this out temporarily before jumping in with both feet? And what if you do fail spectacularly? Couldn't you take that information and explore another option?

Part of the worst-case-scenario exercise is to visualize an actual situation. It's easy to be scared of the unknown because you don't even know what it is! It could be huge! It could bite! It could attack from any direction! But the known? The stuff you can see and name? You can usually find solutions to those fears. Bring them out into the light and think through them.

There is a great chance they are less scary than you think they are.

because they are scared they will be bad at it. This is sort of like being scared the sun will come up tomorrow. *You will for sure be bad at something when you first start*. You won't know how to hold your hands. You'll stumble over your words. You'll get confused. You'll feel awkward and clumsy and may look silly. This is

not something to be afraid of; this is something to expect. Whenever you try something new, you will be starting from scratch, but that doesn't mean you shouldn't do it! That means you should do it right away and get started learning, practicing, and improving. There is no "ready," remember? There is just beginning.

Fitting goals into daily work and life

FITTING GOALS INTO YOUR LIFE is the part that feels the most mystical. How can you achieve this, though? How can you fit all this "bonus" stuff in when the other stuff you are doing is already so time-consuming?

The first thing to do is stop thinking it's magic or that there is a secret solution out there. It's not and there isn't. Once you realize this, you can focus your energy on the time and space that do exist for you.

The second thing is to remember that whatever you're working on might take a while to accomplish as you fit it into your life. That's not a bad thing! That's reality. Could we do everything faster without distractions and setbacks and breaking for meals and sleep? Maybe! But we'd sacrifice so much life, too. Good things take time.

The third thing to keep in mind is that adding the "extra" in is a process. It's not going to go perfectly at first. You may find you have room one week and no room the next. But keep trying. Keep striving to find time for the bonus stuff, because not only will you get better at

fitting it in, it will start to become a part of your routine.

The fourth is that you have to believe that this hobby or goal you want to bring into your life is worthy of your time. Making time and space for creative activities is what makes me "me." There have been periods in my life when being a business owner was the only thing I had room for. There were seasons where motherhood was all consuming. But in normal life and in my average day, my relationships and my business—while huge—are not the only things that are important to me.

That feels uncomfortable to admit. There is this idea that work and parenthood are enough already. Surely you must be phoning it in somehow if you have time for anything else? But I don't believe that we should give up hobbies or stop setting goals and exploring because we have jobs or families. Goals and hobbies are an intricate part of who we are.

And finally, you have to give up the fantasy that "someday" or "next year" or "after retirement" or "when things settle down" is going to

Once you accept that the "perfect day" is not coming, you can stop waiting for it. You can make every day a "good enough day" and begin to work with what you have.

be the solution to making time. That wonderful day in the future when the house is clean and the kids are cared for and the inbox is at zero and the work has been submitted is never coming. *This is sad but also really freeing.* Once you

accept that the "perfect day" is not coming, you can stop waiting for it. You can make every day a "good enough day" and begin to work with what you have.

Breaking
it down

THE BEST THING YOU CAN DO to fit larger projects into your already full days is to break them down into smaller steps. The simpler the step, the better. I like to call these steps *action items*. An action item is a clear, single task that usually can be done in less than thirty minutes. If the action will take longer than thirty minutes, there is a good chance you could break it down even further.

There are a few ways to break things down into action items. Depending on the project, your attention span, and how you like to work, one of these methods may be better for you. Feel free to try them all and see what works for you!

The Recipe Method **involves breaking down all the steps from start to finish in the order that you will do them.** This works great if the steps have to be taken in a specific order or if listing every action item a project entails will help you figure out all the steps you will need to take, regardless of their order.

The Group-by-Task Method **involves thinking about all the similar actions in a certain area.** In my planner, Get To Work Book, I designed a project-breakdown page

around this concept, but you can make your own simply by drawing various boxes on a sheet of paper. Use each box to write similar tasks. I use this method when I am preparing for a craft fair. In one box I'll write items I have to gather from around the office (bulletin boards, pens, clipboard, chair, tablecloth, plant). Another box will hold things I have to package and label (notecards, notepads, prints, planners). Another box will list things I have to make (pricing guide, newsletter sign-up sheet, samples). Then "miscellaneous tasks" (get cash, charge phone, pack car) are listed separately in smaller boxes.

This method is nice because it helps you map out on the page all the different tasks. The order in which you do things isn't very important, but it is important that everything gets done.

The One-Step-at-a-Time Method **involves figuring out what your first step is and getting that done before determining what the next step will be.** I use this method for things I have never tried before. When I sewed my first quilt, I was completely overwhelmed and intimidated by the craft. It seemed to involve a lot of complicated steps and new techniques. Instead of trying to figure them all out (and feeling more discouraged), I bought some fabric. Then I washed and ironed it. Then I cut it. Then I started to sew it into strips, and finally I sewed the strips together. Only once I had a quilt top did I worry about how I was going to get the quilt top combined with the batting and backing fabric. And only after I had completed that did I consider how I would bind the edges.

This method works well when you are diving into something new because it's a slow release of steps and you get the work in batches only when you're ready for it. Even today, after years of knitting and sewing, I rarely read through a full pattern before starting. If I haven't done something like this before, it's unlikely that step 19 is going to make sense to me before I have begun. But after I have completed steps 1 through 18? When I am holding the in-progress pieces in my hands? There is a good chance I am going to be able to understand what to do next.

The value of check-ins

SETTING GOALS AND HAVING A METHOD for breaking them down is important, but equally important is checking in to see where you're at on your progress. I currently spend a few minutes at the end of every month looking back at how the past month went and looking forward to what I am planning to do for the next month.

This exercise is more than just a chance to celebrate what was accomplished (though that's important!) or to see on paper how much is still left to do. It's an opportunity to be sure I am still on board with what I signed up for.

As we talked about last section, so many of our daily activities are just on our list because that's where they have always been. We often forget that we don't have to be doing them or that we can make changes to our schedule. The same is true for goals: sometimes you set a goal (go to grad school, buy a house, and so on) because it makes sense at the time, but then, years later, you find that you are working toward a goal that no longer aligns with who you are or what you want your life to look like.

The truth about goal-setting is that it says more about who you are today than who you

will be in the future. Goal-setting is about your present self making a plan for your future self. But your future self? *They may have a different plan.* They will be a different person. That's good news! That means you are growing and learning and allowing the change to happen.

Don't stick to a plan that doesn't make sense for who you are now. Just because it was the thing you wanted three months ago or three years ago or even three decades ago doesn't make it more valuable.

Each time you do a check-in (either on a specific goal or a few goals at a time), complete the following four steps:

1 **REFLECT ON ANY PROGRESS MADE SO FAR.** What have you done? How did it go? Faster than expected? Slower than expected? Take a moment to celebrate what you did get done.

2 **ASSESS YOUR INTEREST IN THE PROJECT.** Are you still up for this? Do you need to change direction?

3 **RE-EVALUATE YOUR TIMELINE.** Do you think you're still on track to meet this deadline? If yes, great! If not, what do you need? More time for this project? Help with this project? Can you make more space for it in your schedule?

4 **DETERMINE YOUR NEXT STEP OR STEPS.** What would you like to get done in the amount of time before your next check-in? Do you have everything you need for that?

A check-in is an opportunity to take pause for a second and evaluate. It is a chance to be honest about what you actually want and realistic about what can be done. How close are you to actually finishing that? When do you need to start that project? Will you be able to meet that deadline? How would it feel to just let it go?

Revisit your five-year plan

REMEMBER THAT FIVE-YEAR PLAN you wrote out a few pages back? Or that five-year plan you considered writing? Or that five-year plan you started but got overwhelmed by and quit?

Eventually, if you do get to writing it (and I hope you do!), enough time is going to pass that you'll need to revisit it. I like to do an intense check-in on my five-year plan every six months (other times throughout the year, I'll take a look when I am trying to figure out my focuses for the month). Here's what I do each time I sit down again with it:

- **Read through every item with a nonjudgmental eye.** There is a good chance that as time passes some of the stuff you wrote down isn't going to connect with current you. That's okay! That means you are changing. It's likely that some of your goals will now feel irrelevant. Feel free to cross those items off or adjust them so they make sense for who you currently are and what you want.

- **Evaluate your progress.** For the things that do still connect with you, how are you honestly doing? Have you completed anything? Have you made a major dent in anything? As I look at the five-year plan I wrote eleven months ago, only one thing has been "completed" (our shower no longer leaks!), but I am making progress in some areas (I'm currently writing this book, and I have started to make local friends through my book club and an entrepreneur group I started). Take note of any progress you've made and celebrate it.

- **Choose three new action items.** What can you start working on this month to continue moving forward? What would you like to focus on for the next six months?

Something to keep in mind as time goes by and you get closer to your "deadline" of five years is that your objectives may narrow a bit. Of all the things you originally wrote down, you may find you're going to realize just one or two or three of them. That's more than okay. In some ways, I think that's the point. Drafting a five-year plan is sort of like starting college. You have a lot of ideas about who you want to be and the stuff you want to do. And then, as the years go by, you narrow down into the major you want to graduate with and (if you're lucky) determine the field you want to go into. You come out having tried a lot of things and with a better understanding of who you are and what is important to you.

A five-year plan can serve as almost a funnel of ideas. You have a lot of things you want to try and you don't know what exactly will stick, but you're starting somewhere.

Developing a timeline

AN IMPORTANT PART OF WORKING toward any large or long-term goal is having a realistic deadline for when you would like to be done. I find that it's easiest to pick a final (ideal) end date and then work backward to build check-in points within the project.

Sometimes your deadlines will match up with life events. You want to complete X before the baby is born or Y before you move out of the city. Sometimes your end dates line up with the calendar. You want to finish before the end of the year or you need this to be completed before the start of summer. Sometimes a potential end date has nothing to do with an event or season change, so it's up to you to choose a timeframe.

In any case, it's imperative that you're clear on when you want to accomplish your set goal. Without a deadline, this project remains abstract and something that will potentially just sit on your list. If you are not ready to assign an end date to something, keep it off your radar for now. Focus instead on the projects that you can build a clear timeline around.

If your project is not tied to a specific calendar event and you are coming up with your own deadline, be sure to pick something that is realistic (far enough out that it can be accomplished) but also energizing (close enough that you want to get working). Write your date down.

Now, break up the time between today and your ideal finish date. It might be six months away; it might be two weeks away. Divide that timeline up into quarters and make a point to check in on the project when you should be 25 percent through, halfway complete, and 75 percent done—this gives you, starting today, four opportunities to make and evaluate your progress.

If you are not used to self-pacing through projects or tend to finish things right before a deadline, coming up with a timeline may feel like a waste of energy. There is no doubt that a timeline you develop for yourself is arbitrary, and it may be difficult to stay on track when there is no real penalty for meeting your check-in points.

You may be someone who thrives under pressure and you may do your best work at the last minute. If so, that's wonderful! Check-ins and timelines may be useless to you. But if you're someone who would like to space things out or build more of a cushion, try setting the intermediate deadlines and then completing a full check-in with new action items at each step. As with anything, this gets easier with practice. You may find that not feeling stressed toward the end of a deadline or the satisfaction that comes from making progress is reward enough to keep going.

Documenting your progress is informative

WHEN I WAS GROWING UP, my mom kept a frame with nine small boxes, each designed to fit a school picture from kindergarten through eighth grade. I remember looking at that frame in first grade thinking there was no way I'd possibly grow old enough to fill all those boxes. I also remember adding the eighth-grade photo and the joy I felt that it was complete. Looking back on those nine years of photos, I could see growth—I lost baby teeth, I got my ears pierced, I started picking out my own outfits for school picture day, I experimented with how to "style" my hair—this little girl became a teenager, seemingly in moments.

Twenty years later, I am keeping similar frames for my two daughters. I started taking photos of Ellerie when she was six months old against a white wall in our house on New Year's Eve. I have a frame with sixteen holes and ideally, eventually, I'll have sixteen photos of her from age six months to fifteen and a half. This frame will be a neat and tidy progression that seemingly happened in an instant.

Of course nothing changes in an instant. Most changes are gradual and take time. Usually, while we are doing the work (or aging), the progression is so slow it's hard to see that anything is happening. *This is why documenting is so important.*

When we are simply going through the motions of working toward our goal, it can be hard to see that anything is actually happening. As I type this paragraph, I have been writing this book for 107 days. I know I have spent hours upon hours typing and editing, but seeing my word count creep up on the whiteboard next to me is an energy boost and reminder that progress is being made. I have been working on my backyard succulent garden for more than a year. There is still work to be done (is a garden ever *complete*?), but when I compare it to photos from even three months ago, I can see less dirt and more plants, a clear indicator that my time caring for my garden has made a difference.

In addition to being motivating, progress documentation has other values:

DOCUMENTING YOUR PROGRESS CAN BE INFORMATIVE. Often when you see your work you can find patterns. You may notice that one method is more effective than another and you can adjust how you work.

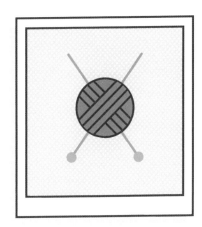

DOCUMENTING YOUR PROGRESS MAKES THE MIDDLE OF A PROJECT MORE EXCITING. Sure, you're not finished, but look at the smaller things that are being accomplished!

DOCUMENTING YOUR PROGRESS IS AN EXERCISE IN GRATITUDE. It provides an opportunity to look back and see how far you have come. It's hard to not be grateful for any progress that you have made when it's right there in front of you.

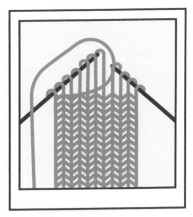

Your goals documentation can take many forms. There is no right way to keep track of progress. You might find that a journal is helpful in providing a space to write down what you did or how you feel. You may find that photos are the most motivating so you can see how you or a project changes over time. You might find that a simple habit tracker (on paper or an app) helps you see progression.

How you document what you're working on is not nearly as important as making the time to document and then reflecting on how things have changed.

Keep a goal tracker
for daily habits

IN 2010 I TRIED A NEW METHOD to track my exercise. It was a simple, single-page calendar with 365 boxes. Each day I completed a workout, I checked a box. It was motivating. Not because I was able to see every day checked off, but because I was able to see how the boxes I did manage to check made up a much larger picture.

I diligently maintained that chart for a year. At the end of a week, I might have been disappointed that I got to the gym only once, but by the end of 2010, I felt as if I had really accomplished something. I could see that on about 30 percent of the days I made an effort to exercise. Even better, I was inspired to do more in 2011.

Since that first year I have kept a daily habit tracker for many activities. I have used one to make sure my family is sitting down at the table for dinner. I have used one to encourage myself to get dressed in something I feel good in. Another one has helped me track making my bed, and I am using one right now to make sure I am getting to a Pilates class a few times a week.

I have heard from many people who have used a daily habit tracker. Some log the days they ate breakfast. Others chart practicing the piano or getting through a load of laundry or reading fifteen pages a day. The goal of the habit tracker is to add *something* to your daily routine. It is to commit to doing one thing until (or even long after) you've established a habit.

As you track your progress in such a visible way, it's possible to step back and see the bigger picture. So you missed a day. Who cares? No big deal. Try again tomorrow. And the day after that. Keep going.

Jerry Seinfeld famously said, "Don't break the chain" when it comes to daily habits and reoccurring tasks. I appreciate the sentiment. Once you've broken the chain and missed a day, it can be easier to miss it again and again. It can be easier to lose sight of the point, because with a missing link, you no longer have a long chain.

But a chain may not be the best metaphor when building a habit or creating a routine. Yes, 100 percent is excellent, but some is still better than none. Instead, a better metaphor than a chain may be a piggy bank. Every day you do the thing, you drop a coin into the piggy bank. If you do something for twenty days, you have twenty coins. But if you miss the twenty-first day, the money already in the piggy bank doesn't disappear. You don't start over with a new bank. If you get back to it on day twenty-two, you now have twenty-one coins. That is still major progress and better than where you started, even if it's not maximal potential.

It's not over if you make a mistake or miss a day. You have still built something. You still have an opportunity to keep building. The best way to think about this is to strive for progress, not perfection. Perfection can be paralyzing. Progress is attainable. It allows for mistakes. It forgives and offers a fresh start.

With a daily habit tracker it's unlikely you'll hit perfection and check off every day (though high-five if you do!), but it's very possible you'll make progress. If you're interested, you can find a free PDF download with 365 days to start your own goal tracker at elisejoy.com/resources.

Flexibility, pivoting, and letting yourself <u>adapt</u>

SOMETIMES THE BEST THING you can do to improve your likelihood of meeting your goal is to lower it. This seems obvious, but this is a step people don't often take before giving up completely. I get it. It's tough to lower the bar and your expectations because in the moment it feels like failure. But instead of thinking that you're "lowering the bar," think about how you're "building a bridge." You're creating a path from where you are right now to where you want to eventually be. This isn't the end of the road—this bridge is a stop along the way.

Let me give you an example:

I started wearing a step tracker about four years ago, and my goal was to get the recommended ten thousand steps each day. I realized that meeting that goal was possible, but I had to reach for it (I had to be sure to take a decent walk or two each day). After about three years of daily wear and mostly meeting my goal, my schedule had changed. I was spending more time at my computer and less time wrangling my kiddos, which resulted in fewer walks and fewer steps. I was lucky to hit five thousand steps by 8 p.m. Ten thousand felt entirely out of reach for my days and lifestyle during this season.

But good news: Because I get to set my own goals, I also get to adjust my own goals. When I realized I wasn't coming close to ten thousand, I dropped my daily step goal to eight thousand. This number was still a stretch, but it was also in the range of possibility. I immediately noticed a difference in my attitude and approach. Suddenly, when it was noon and I saw I was only at fourteen hundred steps, I was motivated to go outside for a quick walk. When it was 7 p.m. and I had six thousand steps, I knew I could make up those two thousand with another short walk or even laps around my house.

I made an adjustment that put my goal back into a realistic range, and because of this I *was willing to reach for it*. I was willing to put forth the effort because I knew the goal was realistic for me.

The results are clear, too: By lowering my own standard, I actually started meeting something higher. After making that goal change, my average step count per day was coming in fifteen hundred steps higher than it was when the goal was more ambitious.

When you adjust your goals, it doesn't mean you can never readjust them back to something bigger. It just means you can set yourself up for potentially greater (albeit maybe slower) success. If eventually you find your new goal overly manageable, then you can change it again. Nothing you do has to be set in stone. Be flexible with yourself. Don't get stuck over something you can change.

I took a yoga class a few years ago and the teacher wore a "BEND, DON'T BREAK" T-shirt. This advice is perfect for yoga and goal-setting. When you become too rigid or set in your ways you will miss opportunities and chances for growth. The most honest thing you can say when it comes to goal-setting is "I have changed" or "This is no longer working for me." Do not associate changing direction with failure! If you don't reach your exact goal but you end up somewhere else, that is still worthwhile and valuable.

Do not associate changing direction with failure! If you don't reach your exact goal but you end up somewhere else, that is still worthwhile and valuable.

Try this
Build mile markers

FOR MANY PEOPLE, the start of a project or the end of a project are usually not as difficult as the middle of a project. How do you keep momentum when the shiny newness has faded but the end is still nowhere in sight? How do you stay focused when it just feels like work? How can you make the middle feel manageable?

During this time period, I like to focus on progress and create my own small victories. As I write this book, I am keeping my word count updated on the whiteboard by my desk. Every addition of one thousand words is a small victory. Every section I edit is a small victory. Being able to see that number go up as this document grows is encouraging.

Can you come up with small victories within your middle? Can you build little landmarks in between the obvious start and end points? I have completed two half marathons and I vividly remember the energy boost at every mile marker. Those stations (usually with smiling, cheering people) were small victories. As I passed each one, my progress felt measurable. While mile markers are obvious for a race (or a road trip), for most projects you will have to construct your own. It's up to you to figure out a way to denote you are moving forward when it feels as if you're stuck in the middle.

Recently, I exchanged emails with a woman who was going through and categorizing tens of thousands of photos. "I am stuck and have no motivation to finish," she lamented.

My recommendation to her was to break up the huge task by creating her own mile markers. For this project, I suggested she think of the remaining photos as groups of two hundred. Then she had to figure out how many groups of two hundred she had left to organize. If it was one hundred groups, she should make a chart with one hundred small boxes. Every time she completed two hundred photos, she could check off one box.

Not only does creating this chart show visual progress, it also gives something more solid to strive for every time she sits down with the photos. She can now think to herself, "I have thirty minutes. I am going to check off four boxes in that time." Then, once the thirty minutes are up and the boxes are checked, she can feel she's completed something. Because she has! She has made progress on this seemingly endless project. Being able to see that makes a difference.

This process can work for any project with no real "end." I use a similar technique when picking weeds from my garden or trying to pull dead leaves off my plants. I am not going to get through all of them today. And by the time I do get through all of them, the first few plants will have dead leaves again. So instead of shooting for "done," my goal is to clear one basket worth of dead leaves and overgrown plants. I can work in the garden for fifteen minutes every few days and know that I am making a difference because I am filling my basket. This method works for laundry, too—you're never done forever unless you move to a nudist colony. So instead of looking to "finish," can you just get through a load a day? Or every few days?

Build yourself those mile markers! Allow yourself the joy of reaching them.

Getting through transitional periods

WHEN LIFE GETS COMPLICATED or you go through a major shift (starting a new job, moving to a new location, having a baby) it's normal and healthy to let your goals sit dormant for a while. In times of transition, your layer 3 activities cannot be your focus because you are relearning how to do layer 2 all over again.

This can be tough.

The most important thing to remember is that what you're currently doing is just a phase. I remember starting a new job at a retail store right out of college. My commute to work involved a car, a train, and a bus. It took an hour each way. I spent my shift on my feet, interacting with customers. When I got home at the end of the day, I was too tired to communicate with my partner, much less think about doing anything extra or creative with my remaining waking hours.

It took about a month to settle into this new schedule. Slowly, my body and brain adjusted to the "new normal." The originally chaotic commute became an opportunity to relax and read.

The constant customer chatter became part of my routine. I completed my training and became comfortable in the store.

Only after all these adjustments were made was I able to find time for "me" projects again. I started crafting again in the evenings or in the mornings when I had the afternoon shift. On my days off I didn't just recuperate from the work-week but began making products to sell in my brand-new Etsy shop.

There is no secret strategy here. You can't rush through the monumental change periods. Instead, you have to brace for them. Expect it to be rough. Expect to feel exhausted. Expect to have little energy for much else. When you're learning something new or starting from scratch, everything you have will be poured into the new experience. This lack of energy is not permanent. It's part of the process. Let it happen! You will be back to feeling like "you," but give it time.

You'll fly somet
you'll fail somet
important, you'
isn't much diffe
the two. When y
learn. When you
When you get t
decision, you ta
know and you t

mes. And
mes. But more
learn there
ence between
ou fail, you
fly, you learn.
the next
e what you
y again.

When it's uncomfortable

I RECENTLY SPOKE WITH A WOMAN who had just launched a new business. She had invested a lot of money in the product line and website and had inventory ready to go but now was struggling to get eyeballs on her product. She wasn't sure if this was something that she was going to be able to make work.

We talked about different marketing techniques she could try, and I recommended a few people I know who often work with similar products. We talked about how this process can be slow but that it doesn't mean that it's bad. We talked about how frustrating it can be to try to find the customer who understands your product's value.

She mentioned that sometimes she lies awake thinking about how nice things were before. She was doing freelance work; it wasn't her dream job, but she was good at it and she had time for her kids, who were just reaching more self-sufficient ages. "Everything was easy! And then I just messed it up!" she joked.

"Right?!" I said. "That's exactly how it always is." You get comfortable with how things are going and so you think, *I have time for this. I have room for this. I can make this work.* And then you go for it. You throw another plate in the air.

But then? *Then you have to juggle that new plate.* Suddenly, this thing you were doing with

ease is hard. You can't take your eyes off it for a second. You can't sit down. You can't take a break. You're in it all over again. And it's hard. All over again.

There is a way to escape this cycle. You don't have to keep adding plates. You can just say "No, thanks" to those Big Ideas. You don't have to change direction or get uncomfortable. And you know what? That's an amazing choice. Being comfortable is a great goal! What a gift to get to a place where you're confident and at peace with what you have going on.

If you're not there yet though and you want to keep adding things, you will go through these uncomfortable phases. You will wonder, "What am I even doing?" You'll question why you ever thought this was a good idea. You'll want to give up. In those moments (or months—sometimes these feelings stick around) I invite you to dig deep. Give your project or adventure everything that you have. It might work out for the best! It might implode! But you'll know something new now. You'll know you tried and you tried hard.

Lying awake and thinking, *This is hard*, is better than lying awake and thinking, *I wonder if I should have tried.*

Dealing with doubt

"I DON'T KNOW HOW TO DO THIS" is a common thought that keeps us from going for something new. We feel doubt and think, *I must not be ready*, but that's false. You're never "ready" to start something new or to make a big change. You hopefully become ready when you're doing the thing.

Another reason we feel doubt is we build up expectation for ourselves that this—this chance, this opportunity, this new idea, this project, this hobby, this time—is it. *This thing* will be the thing that will change it all.

I have good news and bad news. *This thing*? This is not it. There is no *it*. There is never going to be one decision or choice or start or finish that changes everything. There will be good decisions and bad decisions and huge successes and major failures and spectacular launch days and utter flops. All those together will make up *it*. It is life, and life is a process.

When you come to a crossroad, it doesn't matter if you go left or right. If you go left and it works—great! Keep going. There is a new crossroad up ahead and you'll be choosing again shortly. If you go left and it doesn't work—great! Walk back to the crossroad and start down the other path. You learned something by going down that left path that you can now apply to the next crossroad just up ahead.

You can feel doubt. You can double-check and reconfirm and take your time and hem and haw. It's all allowed. But spending that time doubting right now will not make it any easier to follow through once you've decided what to do. You will become better at dealing with doubt by doing things *despite* doubt. You'll fly sometimes. And you'll fail sometimes. But more important, you'll learn there isn't much difference between the two. When you fail, you learn. When you fly, you learn. When you get to the next decision point, you take what you know and you try again.

"But wait!" you might say. "Elise, I don't think you understand. My doubt over this is unbearable and I can't do it."

"No worries! Don't do it!"

Let me be clear: If the doubt you are feeling is all consuming, you don't have to do this thing! Don't keep stuff you're never going to do because of fear on your list. Don't let those ideas float around and take up space in your brain. It's stressful to live with doubt and fear. There are enough real things to be scared of to let your goals (which should be fun and exciting) cause panic. If you're not ready and you don't want to just try anyway, then let it go. Write that thing you just can't do right now down on a piece of paper and tuck it away. Maybe you'll never do it. Maybe five years from now you'll take the plunge. Either way—you're going to be okay.

When you stop working toward something that doesn't interest you or excite you, you don't lose. You gain! You gain the time and energy to find the thing that you're actually going to connect to.

When is it okay to <u>stop?</u>

I STOP THINGS ALMOST AS FREQUENTLY as I start things. The only reason I see anything to completion is because I start *a lot* of things.

The key is figuring out *why* you want to stop working on something. Ask yourself these questions:

IS THIS TOO DIFFICULT? Have you chosen to work toward something that is impossible right now? Maybe the time, money, or resources simply don't line up. If so, would you want to adjust? Could this project be successful if it was smaller? Or if the materials were different? Or if you reduced your commitment ? If you set the deadline further in the future, could you reach it?

ARE YOU BORED? Have you become so used to this project that it is no longer inspiring or exciting? Can you change it in some way? Narrow your focus? Expand on your focus? Maybe this project or goal is too easy for you. Can you make it more of a challenge? Is there anything you can think of that would recharge your energy for this?

DO YOU WANT TO DO THIS? You may have started this project or began working toward this goal because you felt you should, not because you actually wanted to. This almost never works out. You don't have to enjoy every step of the process, but if you don't *want* to get this done, you're not going to get this done. That's okay.

If you can't change a goal or project into something that makes sense for you, let it go. We have this bizarre mindset as a culture that to quit is to fail. I reject that on every level. *To quit is to get closer to what is actually right for you.* When you stop working toward something that doesn't interest you or excite you, you don't lose. You gain! You gain the time and energy to find the thing that you're actually going to connect to. Quitting is an opportunity to figure out what will be a better fit.

There is no "made it," and what that means for continuing your work

WHAT HAPPENS WHEN YOU FINISH a project or meet your goal? When I finally do the thing I set out to do, I often find I am relieved but also a bit underwhelmed. The "I did it!" feeling is often followed by a feeling of "Hmm, that was it?"

Yep! *That was it.*

We hear "It's the journey, not the destination" so often that it's become a frustrating cliché. When you're on the journey—climbing the hill, running the race, getting through the night with a newborn—the future "destination" looks pretty spectacular. The idea of being "done" can become consuming. Which is good! Keeping that finish line in sight is motivating and helps you finish the project.

Early in my career, when I was figuring out how to work for myself, I kept thinking there would be *A Moment*. The moment that would launch me and my business. Maybe it would be *this* project. Or maybe it would come from *this* collaboration. Or maybe if I just made *this* amount of money. I'd be there!

And then I would complete that project. I would do that collaboration. I'd hit that financial goal. And, of course, I was still me, now with an extra line in my bio and a few more dollars in the bank. This isn't to say that I wasn't glad to have done the thing. It isn't to say I wasn't satisfied with how things were going. Nope. What it means is that wherever you go, whatever you do, there *you* are.

Most likely when you finish that project or reach your goal, you'll feel joy and elation and pride—you did it! But don't be surprised if you also feel a tinge of a letdown. You did it! And, wait for it, *you're still you*. You're the same person today (a finisher!) as you were yesterday (a work in progress!). This is because no matter what you get done, *you* will remain a work in progress. Always.

When you complete a project or reach a milestone, take time to celebrate it. Celebrations look different for everyone. You might throw a giant party or you might take a quiet day off to read in bed. Do the thing that makes you feel good.

After I reach a goal, I feel lost for a few days without the structure and momentum of working toward something. I often find that the next few things I attempt don't click for me because I am either trying too hard to make them be the "next big thing" or I am phoning it in for something to do.

For me, it's important to acknowledge this period. I like to experiment and recharge. I will often take time to look at my current five-year plan and think about the three-things concept and how I can find some smaller items to work on while I rebalance.

When one project ends and you're looking around for the next thing to focus on, the most important thing to remember is this: You have had good ideas before and you'll have good ideas again. There is no rush! You are a work in progress. ➤➤

- *share some of the lessons I have learned in ten years of working toward goals*
- *encourage you to reject the inspiration cycle and make peace with the highlight reel*
- *help you rethink your relationship to email*
- *give you a "non-guilt trip"*
- *invite you to sit down with me for a cup of coffee*
- *not be able to explain how to win the lottery*
- *stand up for failure*

Part 4

Let's Get It Done

To get the work done, you gotta do the work.

You gotta do the work

I MENTIONED THAT ONE OF MY GOALS years ago was to bake forty loaves of different types of bread. This was one of those challenges where it's easy to get distracted. I could convince myself that combing recipes on Pinterest was getting me closer to my goal. Or I could spend money on fancy bread trays or new cookbooks and justify these purchases as necessary to meet my goal. But the reality was that to complete this challenge, I had to do just one thing: I had to bake the bread.

You gotta do the work.

It's exactly that simple and that complicated.

Because of course you have to do the work! But the work itself is often hard and repetitive and boring. It's easier and more fun to spend time doing all the things that are on the periphery of the work, such as getting organized, brainstorming, or gathering inspiration. This is the case for almost any craft, but I think it's especially true of writing. You hear all the time that if you want to be a good writer, you have to read a lot. (I think this is true.) Reading provides access to new ideas. It helps you figure out what you like and don't like. It can help you home in a bit on your own style.

But you know what *really* makes a good writer? Someone who writes.

My favorite public challenge is one I will probably never partake in: NaNoWriMo, November's National Novel Writing Month. The goal is to write fifty thousand words in one month, or basically to write a book in thirty days. A nonprofit organization exists to help turn hundreds of thousands of people into novelists by encouraging them sign up, check in, track their progress, and support one another, but, most important, to—yes—write.

This is a big challenge—fifty thousand words is a lot of words—but it's not an impossible challenge, and it's something that can be done if you sit down and write that novel. To bake forty loaves of bread, you have to mix the ingredients, knead the dough, and turn on the oven. To write fifty thousand words, you have to sit down and type them out.

To get the work done, you gotta do the work.

The other stuff, finding the inspiration or the perfect tools or clearing the time, is a distraction from the real task: doing the work.

Reject the "inspiration cycle"

I WAS AT AN EVENT A FEW YEARS AGO where author Scott Berkun talked about the inspiring story loop (though I am not sure that's exactly what he called it) and about how people tend to look for the feel-good story or the inspirational message before they get motivated to sit down to work. Then, when they do sit down to finally work, they notice that the work doesn't "feel good" or seem "inspirational," so they think they must be doing something wrong. Fearful that this isn't how the work is supposed to feel, people will assume it must be time to hear another story or read another motivational quote. This cycle can go on and on and is hard to break.

Scott reminded the audience that when you're sitting at your desk or doing the task and you're telling yourself, "this isn't fun," *that's when you really start working.* That's when you're finally doing the work that will someday be your own inspiring story.

I found myself nodding along. I have done this. I have spent plenty of time in the "inspiration cycle." Browsing other people's feeds.

Scrolling miles of Pinterest. Looking at his images. Reading her stories. I have found myself valuing the already completed work of others more than my own in-progress work.

We all contribute to the "inspiration cycle." No matter what you're doing—getting an education, raising kids, handling insurance claims, writing books, trying cases, building bridges, making sense of spreadsheets, teaching students, growing veggies, managing financial operations, building wells in Africa—you're contributing.

And we all consume the "inspiration cycle." All day, every day, we consume. There is nothing wrong with taking in information. There's nothing wrong with fist-pumping at someone else's inspiring story or tearing up over someone else's breakthough. It's part of the process and certainly not a bad thing.

But the trick, when you're trying to do something different, is to pay attention to the ratio. Are you spending three hours looking at other peoples' work and only one hour on your own? Can you flip that equation? Three hours for you, just one hour for others?

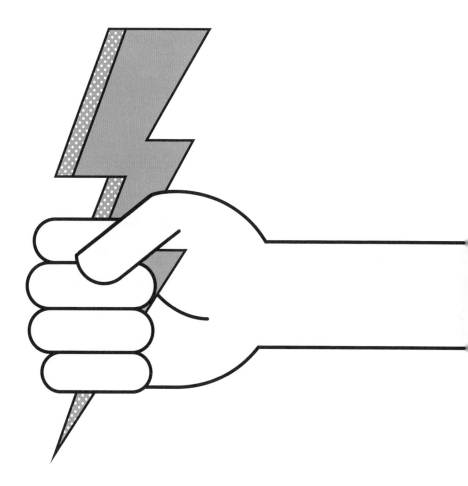

Your best work will be something that you do, not something that happens to you. It will not fall from the sky. Lightning won't strike. The light bulb will not click on. Instead, *you must go to the work*. You need to chase the lightning down. You need to flip the lights on and off until they stay lit.

This may not feel good. It may not feel inspiring. It may feel as if you're moving in circles. That's okay. Don't avoid or fight this feeling! It means you are getting something real done.

The more time you spend consuming, the less time you will have to create. And the more time you spend reading the stories of others, the less time you have to write your own.

You want to make stuff? Make it. You want to write stuff? Write it. You want to do something different? Do it. Get in and be inspired, but then get out! *And then get to work*.

Your best work w[ill]
that you do, not s[omething]
happens to you. [...]
the sky. Lightnin[g ...]
The light bulb wi[ll ...]
Instead, you mus[t ...]
You need to chas[e ...]
down. You need t[o ...]
on and off until t[he ...]

l be something
mething that
will not fall from
won't strike.
not click on.
go to the work.
the lightning
flip the lights
ey stay lit.

Handling the highlight reel

I CAN'T TALK ABOUT THE "INSPIRATION CYCLE" without talking about the constant highlight reels we scroll through daily online.

I started my blog in 2005. I was twenty and a junior in college. Social networking wasn't what it is today, so a blog was often where you went to share online. I became an adult while documenting my life online. I took finals. I interned for companies. I interviewed for jobs. I graduated college. I moved across the country to live with my boyfriend. I got a job at a retail chain. I started an online Etsy shop. I got engaged. I planned a wedding. I got married. I moved back across the country. I planted a garden. I sent my husband on deployment. I welcomed him home. I got pregnant. I sent my husband on another deployment. I bought a house. I had gestational diabetes. I had a baby. I struggled through a period of postpartum depression. I got better. I tried many business ideas. I started a podcast. I launched Get To Work Book. I got pregnant again.

Throughout all this I had bad days and good days. I felt insecure. I felt on top of the world. I worried about money. I celebrated big milestones. I fought with my husband. I fought with my kids. I lived ten years of my life! And I shared just fractions online of what that offline life looked like.

I am lucky that I got in the blog game early and had a chance to go through so much personal transition as a content creator. I have written the blog posts that gloss over the mundane to highlight the magic. I have pushed the mess off the counter and out of the frame to take a photo to post to Instagram. I have told the sweet story about my cute kid, while not telling the story about when she screamed and cried and told me she wanted "a new mom."

I know that I am choosing what stories to tell and what photos to share. Because of this, I know that other people—yep, even that one woman with the "perfect life"—are doing the same thing online. Everyone loses their patience. Everyone feels lost. Everyone has self-doubt. *We have to understand this.* There is no secret here. Finding out that so-and-so also has bad days and feels sad/insecure/inadequate/boring should not come as a surprise or make us feel better. *Of course so-and-so does. She's human.*

I once had a great boss who said everyone should work in retail and food service for a year to see what's it's like to be on the other side of customer service. (I agree!) In the social media age, everyone should share photos of their lives online for a year. The goal is not to learn to be more compassionate online (though that would be a great bonus). The goal is to see that you're making choices about what you're sharing. You're going to hide some stuff! You're going to highlight other stuff. And you're going to realize that everyone else is doing that, too.

The Highlight-Reel Desk

The Real Desk

Don't hoard ideas

I USED TO FEAR WASTING IDEAS. I worried that if I did something, that activity or idea or opportunity would be "used up." And what if, weeks later, I came up with a better solution? Or worse, what if, weeks later, I really needed an idea but I had already used them all?

I now know my concern was ridiculous. Running out of ideas is not a thing that can happen.

You cannot waste ideas, because they are not a zero-sum game. The more you create, the more ideas you will have. The more you experiment, the more you'll want to learn. The more answers you find, the more questions you will have. This is good news, but until you have really practiced it, it can be hard to believe.

One project I completed that really helped me "see" this in action was when I tried to find one hundred ways to get plants on fabric during one of my hundred-day projects. I gave myself strict rules: each day I had to work with fabric (at least a six-by-six-inch square), and the fabric had to incorporate plants. For one hundred days I quilted, stitched, painted, embroidered, dyed, hammered, sewed, puff-painted, and somehow got plants on

fabric. In the beginning the project felt absurd. How was I going to do this? Could I really come up with enough ideas to keep this interesting?

And ninety-nine days later, when the project ended, I felt overwhelmed by the possibilities. There are millions of plants in the world. I was able to capture only a tiny fraction. There are thousands of ways to embellish fabric. I was able to try only a few of them. There are limitless colors and color combinations. I was able to work with only some.

Every day as I worked on this project, I had an idea for something else I could try. That next idea would never have come to me if I had sat still with a piece of paper and a pencil and tried to pull an idea from thin air. The new ideas came because I got engaged and started creating.

Making breeds making. The best way for you to have an idea is to start on another idea. The best way for you to find a great solution is to try an okay solution. You need to be active in your idea-making. You must keep your eyes open, yes, but also your hands moving and your brain engaged.

Making breeds making. The best way for you to have an idea is to start on another idea. The best way for you to find a great solution is to try an OK solution. You need to be active in your idea-making.

The value of first drafts and idea dumps

ONE OF THE THINGS that seems to hold people back from simply starting a new project or trying a new idea is the fear that the end result will not be perfect, or there will be missteps and errors along the way.

To that I say, "Of course!" The end result will absolutely not be perfect and many things will go wrong as you take an idea and turn it into something real. This is going to happen, and it's important that you accept that from the beginning and stop fearing it.

As I worked on my plants-on-fabric project, I had days when I created something I loved and days when I hated the results. About halfway through the project, I looked back on my previous work and decided to redo the squares that were bugging me. My only requirement was that the new fabric squares had to be "inspired" by the original squares. I wanted them to reflect my work from the original day, but I wanted to love them.

It had taken me five days to create the original pieces, and I was able to replace them all in about two hours. These squares that had left me feeling underwhelmed and had been declared "good enough, I guess" were now exciting (and easy!) to re-create.

Why is this?

The original ideas were rough drafts. They were created from nothing. I had to pull them to the surface and complete them. The new attempts got to use the drafts as a springboard and only had to be tweaked. *Once you have a rough draft or sample, it's easier to make changes or corrections because it already exists.* This concept is now real. It might be terrible, but at least when it's terrible you have something to improve on. You can do the opposite of the concept now. You can build it out. You can fix it. You can edit it into something that works.

It's much easier to know how you feel about something that exists. It's easier to say, "No, I don't like that," to something you can see. It's hard to make something out of nothing, but it's imperative to the process, because once you get that initial idea out there, you can mold, shape, cut, paste, hammer, and sew it into something better.

Try this
Pick a "just do it" day

WHEN I WAS GROWING UP, my dad would often ask my brother and me to do something we didn't want to do by saying, "This is going to take hours and it will be boring and terrible." At the time, it made me angry, but I also couldn't help but feel amused at the absurdity of his "motivational speech." Now, I think it was a brilliant strategy. Some things *are* boring and terrible and they do take a long time. That doesn't mean we get to skip them . . . it means we have to gear up and power through them.

As an adult I do a version of the same thing and set up "just do it" days for myself. I tell myself in advance this day will be terrible and boring and then I make a list of things I have been dreading or putting off and crank through it. It is always terrible and boring, but it's so much better than letting the dread linger. The best part of these days is that you are able to build momentum as you cross stuff off, and it's rewarding to complete everything you have been avoiding for so long.

Finding motivation

SO, YOU HAVE THE IDEA. You know your next step. You want to do this. But you can't seem to get started, either on the entire project or on the progress that you need to make today. What then?

The first thing to remember is that you can build motivation the way you would build any muscle: through practice and exercise. Motivation often feeds on momentum! Once you get started and begin to see the results of your effort, it will get easier and easier to maintain your motivation. If you have struggled to feel motivated for years, don't panic! You have an opportunity to change your story.

Here are a few things to try.

CLEAR LITERAL SPACE. I find that cleaning off my desk, taking out the trash, or sweeping the floor can help me get in the right zone to start working.

CREATE A RITUAL. Come up with a short routine (taking five deep breaths, doing a handstand, pouring a fresh cup of coffee, saying a prayer) that you can do before you dive into the work. This ritual can be the cue or trigger that tells you it's time to get started.

TELL YOURSELF IT'S JUST A TRIAL RUN. Whatever you have to do today is just practice and a warm-up. Don't worry about it being perfect or even your best; focus instead on getting *something* done.

SET A TIMER. Give yourself ten minutes (just ten minutes!) to work right now. You can do anything for ten minutes—even pretend you feel motivated.

These small actions work as bridges between you feeling unmotivated and you doing the work. Motivation can sometimes be overrated. Yes, of course it would be great to feel ready and raring to go each day, but the people who get things done get them done because they do the work even when they don't feel motivated. Often I find that my motivation comes *while* I am working, not before I start working. It's normal that I have to trick myself into starting.

Here is what you shouldn't do when you lack motivation or energy:

Go looking for inspiration. What you need to get moving is already inside of you. You've got this already. It's there. Get out of the way, stop scrolling, and start working.

The best tool is the one you'll use

MY JOB IS TO SELL A PLANNER, and so I am often asked, "Why is this the best planner?" My answer always starts the same way: "I don't know if this is the best planner for you, but here are the features that make it different." I think Get To Work Book is great! But because it deserves to serve as more than a paperweight, I also use my sales pitch to remind people that if they already have a system—whether it's an app, a notebook, a wall calendar, or a spreadsheet—and it works for them, then they are set.

If it's broke, fix it! But if it's not broke, stop worrying about it and just use it.

I started writing this book in a Google Doc and I am finishing it in Microsoft Word. Every few days someone asks me where I am writing the book and every few days someone recommends Scrivener, which is a writing software program that is designed to help writers organize their thoughts and their books.

Before I started writing I went to the Scrivener website to check out this "must use" tool. It looks amazing! It looks like it has great features! It looks like it could be very helpful. It also made me anxious and overwhelmed. Now, in addition to writing this book, it looked like I would need to learn a new program.

I had two choices. I could download this new program. I could take the time to learn it. I could get familiar with it. I could start writing my book.

Or, I could open up a Google Doc and start writing my book. I chose the latter.

"Looking for the right tool for the job" is actually a great way to avoid "doing the job." You can quickly convince yourself that to do this project correctly you need something special. But often to do this project correctly, you just need to do it.

I am not saying that you shouldn't look for the right tool for the job or that you shouldn't try to find new and better ways to do things. I am saying that if what you do have works, then use it. Spending a week looking for the most aerodynamic hammer that feels great in your hand when you have one nail to get into the wall is just a form of procrastination.

All the tools—even the very best tools—are useless if you are not comfortable using them. It doesn't matter if you have the fanciest car if you don't know how to drive. It doesn't matter if you have a beautiful pool if you can't swim. It's wonderful if you use Scrivener and it works for you! It's also wonderful if you use a pencil and write out your novel by hand! The point is that you've found *your* tool. The one that works for you is the best tool.

If it's broke, fix it! But if it's not broke, stop worrying about it and just use it.

Treat your email inbox as a communication tool

YOUR EMAIL INBOX should serve as a communication tool. Not a storage unit. Not entertainment. Not a to-do list. It shouldn't be a place of stress or anxiety. You should feel about email the way you feel about your stapler: *this is something that sits on my desk that performs a task.* That task is communicating.

If you love email and checking your inbox is a joy, that's amazing. But if you are struggling under a mountain of email and want to get out from under it, let me share a few things that may help you get there.

To start, repeat after me: The purpose of email is to communicate with people. With that in mind, here are a few tips for dealing with email.

PREVENT UNNECESSARY EMAILS FROM COMING IN. Start by unsubscribing from the newsletters you never open anyway. This clears space so that you are able to see the real stuff you do want and need to open. If you have a business or frequently answer the same questions via email, set up a great FAQ page that addresses those common questions. Not only will this help you avoid some email traffic, it will be faster and easier for your customers to get the answers they need.

OPEN YOUR INBOX ONLY WHEN YOU ARE PREPARED TO MAKE DECISIONS. This is a big one. Don't let your email inbox be something you casually open and scroll. If you're casually scrolling, you're not in the right mindset to respond. If you're

not able to respond, you're not communicating. When you are answering emails, you are making choices (Can you attend? When can you meet? Will you do this?) or you are taking action (sending that file, checking on that report, paying that bill). If you don't have the time to make those choices or take those actions, don't open your inbox.

USE THE ARCHIVE FEATURE. Once you have read and responded to an email (or decided that you are not going to respond), archive it! Clear it from your inbox! It will still exist in your email storage but it will not clutter up that communication space. The next time you open your inbox, you will not have to see something you've already handled. How you file things is up to you, but in most cases, I have found the search feature to be good enough in helping me find what I need to find after it's been archived.

PICK UP THE PHONE. How much time are you willing to spend on a single email? Ten minutes? Twenty? My limit is about ten minutes, and if it's going to take me longer to write the email or draft the response, it's time to call the person. If you don't know the person well enough to call them, then consider simplifying (and shortening!) your email. Remember, if you don't know them, they do not know you. A shorter email that gets straight to the point is what the person on the receiving end will be looking for.

WRITE IT DOWN. If an email comes through with information for a future date, don't store that email in your inbox until the future date. Write it down or add it to your calendar and then archive the email! On the day of the event you can pull it up again if you need it, but don't let it clutter your inbox every moment from now until then.

DECLARE BANKRUPTCY. Do you have hundreds of emails in your inbox, some months old that are waiting for a response? Are you going to get to those emails? If yes, good. Pick a day and clear your schedule and start hammering them out. But if no, that's also good. Delete them and start fresh. Then commit to doing the five things above from here on.

And finally, if none of this works for you and you are not getting back to the folks who email you, it might be time to admit that you shouldn't use email. This may seem crazy. "Everyone uses email to communicate! I can't not email!" But if you're not responding within a reasonable timeline, *you already are not using email.* You're just pretending that you use email. Which is even worse. I would rather get an auto-response within a minute from a person that says, "Hey! I don't use email; I will never get back to you about this," than never hear back. In both cases I don't get an answer to my inquiry, but in only one case am I left hanging.

Being **honest** about who you are

WHAT DO YOU LIKE TO DO? What are you good at? What do you dislike? What are you not good at? You don't have to tell me (or anyone!) the answers to these questions, but you should know the answers.

We live in a FOMO world with access to *all* of the things, ideas, and opinions. Because we spend so much time taking this all in, sometimes our own personal thoughts, ideas, wants, and needs are neglected.

It's easy to compare what you are doing to what someone else is up to. Or to read a critique before you've seen a movie or a Yelp review before you try the restaurant. This is potentially great (maybe you'll save yourself ninety minutes or subpar service) but also terrible because it means you are holding the opinions of someone else in higher regard than you hold your own.

People talk often of "guilty pleasures" or things they do despite the fact that they are not held in high regard. Reject the concept of "guilty pleasures." Unless what you love to do is commit crimes or harm yourself or others, you need to stop having guilt about the things that bring you joy.

Do you like correcting typos on *Wikipedia* articles? Watching slime videos? Hand-stitching quilts? Making one hundred Christmas cards? Great. It doesn't matter if someone else thinks what you are doing is a waste of time. If you enjoy it, if you finish those thirty minutes or thirty hours and feel good—that's an excellent use of your time. No guilt.

After giving yourself permission to do the small stuff you enjoy—think bigger. What is it that you want from life? An empire? A steady paycheck? A movie career? Do you want a sprawling farm? A home on wheels? A place in a big city? There are no wrong answers as long as you are being honest with yourself. If you know what you want, it is so much easier to avoid FOMO and cultivate FOFSED (fear of following someone else's dreams).

I don't want to run an empire (I don't even want full-time employees). I want a job that is challenging, but I also want time for the hobbies I love. I want to spend the majority of my weekends and weeknights at home with my kids and husband. I want, on occasion, to have adventures, but I also know I love to be home. For me, *this is the dream*. But your dream could and probably will look different. That doesn't make mine right or yours right. It means we are doing life right—we are being honest about what we want.

In her book, *Yes Please*, Amy Poehler summed it up perfectly: "Good for her, not for me."

When someone is doing something differently from or even opposite of how you do it—see it as an opportunity. You can look at this other option and think, *Wow, so many things are possible*, and then move forward on your own path. You don't have to change your method or your direction, and instead you can take comfort in the fact that there is no "right" way. The constant quest for the "right way" is what keeps us from enjoying "our way."

Try this
Let it go

THERE IS A GOOD CHANCE you are carrying around with you a lot of extra stuff that doesn't matter. You've picked it up along the way because someone said you should or five years ago it was your favorite or everyone said it was worth it. This can be literal stuff, products that were recommended or trends you tried, but it can also be negative self-talk, toxic relationships, or ideas that are not going to pan out.

Let it go.

Holding tightly to the stuff that isn't working is like letting a black cloud hang over you and the things that do really matter—the products you do love, the wonderful relationships, and the good ideas. Make some space.

What about the <u>really</u> hard stuff?

"ELISE," YOU MIGHT BE THINKING RIGHT NOW, "this is helpful advice if you're feeling good. I understand how a handstand and clear desk might build a motivational bridge. But what about when I am really struggling? What about the anxiety? Depression? Loss? Grief? How do I begin to think about building a normal schedule or dreaming bigger in the midst of these issues?"

I hear you. I am grateful that you picked up this book amid those feelings. I am fearful of writing the wrong thing, so I am going to pretend that we are friends and sitting down for coffee in real life. This is what I would say to you:

I don't have a solution for how to deal with everything huge and awful that can occur. I do know that in the times when I have felt my weakest and the most underwater, I had two choices. I could cry out for help or I could continue to sink.

As a thirteen-year-old, while suffering abuse from a school bully, I waited months before I finally broke down and told my story to a guidance counselor. By the end of that period, I didn't recognize myself; I was so riddled with anxiety, but reaching out was the first step to regaining my confidence.

As a junior in college, while struggling with the beginnings of an eating disorder, I had a friend recommend, just in time, that I schedule an appointment with a school nutritionist. After a few meetings with her, I was able to start working through my issues with food. Years later I still think back to what I learned from my talks with her, and I am so grateful I met her as quickly as I did.

As a new mom, while adjusting to my new role, I failed to reach out for help because I was scared of being misunderstood, and I almost drowned.

When Ellerie was born, I fell into a depression that lasted just over a year. Depression looks different for everyone. For me, it felt like helplessness and it looked like crying. I cried every day. I cried in the shower. I cried on the phone with my mom whenever we spoke. I cried in the car with my dad on Easter Sunday while looking for a parking spot in Santa Monica. I cried while playing with Ellerie. I cried when Paul got home from work late. I cried before getting out of bed. I cried while falling asleep. I cried thinking about how much I was crying.

I want to fly back in time and tell myself that I will be okay. I also want to tell myself to start screaming for help. I want to tell myself that this is temporary but that it's necessary that I find someone to talk to who knows what they are doing and can help me begin to work through this.

Whenever I find myself in a tough season, it's impossible to look forward, because I am just trying to get through this minute. If I can do this minute, I might be able to handle the next. And if I get through more minutes, eventually I will get through this hour. You might relate to this, or your journey might be entirely different. I so wish that I had magic words to make things better. Many more people have been through worse than me and have written so much more eloquently about this topic. I wish they were here, having coffee with us, so I could listen and learn alongside you.

I believe that working through this and shouting for help is worth it. The world needs you. Your voice. Your perspective. Your talent and, yes, your challenges. Please reach out. I understand how hard it can be to do. There is no weakness here. You don't have to carry anything alone.

Putting your-
self out there

I WAS LISTENING TO A PODCAST a few years ago (most of my best stories start like this), and one of the hosts talked about a conference he went to called XOXO. It had been a weekend of speakers who had created something great on the internet, each sharing their "path to success" and recommending ways to get traffic or hits or "make it big," as they had.

The last guy, Darius Kazemi, got up and said, "Hey, today I want to talk to you about how I won the lottery." And then he flashed his numbers up on the screen and proceeded to explain that the secret was picking the nines and threes and so on.

Do you get it?

Breaking down the steps for how you create a viral video or write a bestseller or have an idea that shakes up an industry is a lot like explaining how you won the lottery.

Winning the lottery is (in some cases) picking the nines and the threes and so on. But it's also . . . buying the ticket. It's potentially buying lots of tickets. It's knowing when the lottery closes and which vendor is the closest to your work. It's also next to impossible, but it's easy not to dwell on that.

Just as there is no secret to picking the winning lottery numbers, there is no formula that you can follow or book you can read to make things turn out well. Here is what you can do: you can show up.

You can put yourself out there. You can make and share *hundreds* of ideas, and maybe one of them will get picked up by the right Twitter star and your project will go viral. You write and you write and you write and maybe someday Oprah's intern will read your book and leave it by her desk and she will pick it up and love what you wrote and make it her book club pick.

At XOXO Darius went on to say:

What I've learned is that—beyond a certain level of effort—there's basically no correlation between the amount of work you put into something and how successful it is. At least for me.

There's not much that you can control about your creative success once you've actually made the thing. And, in a sense, there are two kinds of creative advice that I think you can get from creative people. The first is how to buy more lottery tickets. And the second is how to win the lottery. I think the former can be extremely useful, and I think the latter is nonsense.

You can't control the lottery or the internet or Oprah. But you can control how many ideas you're putting out there. You can keep sharing. You can keep buying the tickets. Do that.

Try this
Try a daily creative challenge

A FEW YEARS AGO, I watched Trevor Noah interview John Oliver on *The Daily Show*. Noah hosts his show on weeknights while Oliver hosts his show *Last Week Tonight* on Sundays. They joked about whose job is harder—the nightly host or the weekly host—and Oliver said, "There is a great mental clarity to having a show to do the next day because then you don't feel too bad about the show you've just done."

They laughed, as if this was a dig on Noah's show and how often he may be delivering "bad" shows, but I found the point perfectly stated. When you're performing nightly, you can't get too caught up on how the show went last night. When you are playing the baseball game, you can't think too hard about the ball you just dropped because you have to catch the next one that is coming your way. When you are creating daily work, you can't overthink the work you created today because you have to do it again tomorrow.

The fact that you made something you didn't love today doesn't matter when you have to make something again tomorrow. This is the power of daily creative projects. You can't dwell because you have to keep going.

So much of life is taking a swing. In the rush to compare home runs and take a selfie on first base,

this gets forgotten. You will spend most of your life just going up to bat. That's it. Sometimes you strike out. Sometimes you get a walk. Sometimes you hit foul ball after foul ball. Sometimes you bunt to advance another runner. But you're playing. You're up there. You're doing it. You're not just swinging for the fences.

This is how you get more comfortable creating work and sharing work. This is how you get more comfortable with things not going as planned or not being your "best" work. You keep creating. You keep making. You don't stop because it's hard.

At the end of your creative project, whether you did it for one hundred days or a month or a year, you don't just have the "things" that you have created. You have the perspective that came from "doing the things." You learned that you could do this. You learned that when you made something less than great, it was still okay. You saw that making one thing gave you an idea for making another thing. You saw that when you pushed, you got it done.

This is the power of the daily creative project: the ability that it has to shape your attitude about your work. Your art might not get better. But you will get better at making art.

Just as there i
picking the wi
numbers, ther
that you can f
you can read t
turn out well. I
you can do: yo

no secret to
ning lottery
is no formula
llow or book
make things
ere is what
can show up.

It doesn't have to be flawless to be complete

MY DAD'S FAVORITE PHRASE IS "Perfection is not flawlessness, it's wholeness and completeness." He thinks he heard it in a motivational speech by a *National Geographic* photographer in 1994. I found a similar quote from Marion Woodman in her 1928 book *Addiction to Perfection*: "Perfection is defeat . . . Perfection belongs to the gods; completeness or wholeness is the most a human being can hope for."

Either way it is a—for lack of a better word—perfect reminder.

You can't be perfect. Your project can't be perfect. Your house, life, goals, job, kids, marriage, friendships, routines, hair, and body cannot be perfect. You will be flawed. You will make mistakes and tear holes and have fights and miss deadlines and get scars and stain your carpet. You will also cry tears of joy and create work you're proud of and make love and see a sunset and develop laugh lines and sing along to your favorite song and eat a great meal.

This is perfection. It's the wholeness and completeness of life. It's that dance between the crappy and the wonderful. Accepting that you are going to always have a bit of both is why you are here. Life is not a quest to "do it all exactly right" or to never admit or acknowledge your flaws, but to instead keep going anyway.

The quest for perfection is not only impossible, it's a hindrance. You may think, *I can't do this perfectly, so I am not doing it at all*. Or, *I can't do everything, so I am not going to do some*. This thinking is how you lose. *I can't stop the polar ice caps from melting, so why recycle this can? I'll be moving from this house in eighteen months, so why hang a photo on the wall? I didn't eat a healthy lunch, so why eat a healthy dinner? I can't make time to run every day, so why run Tuesdays and Thursdays?*

Do these examples feel extreme? Are they exactly on target? How often have you told yourself there is no point in doing something because you aren't good enough at it or because you might mess it up?

So much gets wasted on the quest for perfection. If we spent any of this time, energy, and focus just doing the task, we would be so much closer to building something whole and complete.

So much gets wasted on the quest for perfection. If we spent any of this time, energy, and focus just doing the task, we would be so much closer to building something whole and complete.

TENTH ANNUAL

You Learned Something!

CERTIFICATE OF EFFORT

THIS IS NOT YOUR THING

ALMOST!

YOU TRIED!

Presented with

A CHANCE *to* START OVER

CONGRATULATIONS

This is not the End of the World

Let's talk about failure

THERE IS A POPULAR PHRASE: "What would you do if you knew you couldn't fail?" (I just Googled it and got 54 million results.) I would like to find and replace them all with:

What would you do if you knew that failure wasn't the end of the world?

It's time to get over this idea that "failure" should be avoided at all costs. If you believe that—if you believe that failure is bad, you will not try. Failure is not great, but it's definitely not bad! It's just part of doing something. The best way to avoid failure is to never try, so if you are too scared to fail, you will be too afraid to try.

Don't protect yourself from failure. Get comfortable with it. Failure is a chance to start over and rebuild or adjust.

I use the words *failure* and *fail* often, especially with my creative projects. I will casually state, "Oh, that idea failed." Or, "This is either going to be really great or will fail." I am comfortable with the word but often find that others are not. They are quick to respond with something like, "You didn't fail, you learned something!" which

is almost correct. "I did fail, so I learned something." Yes, it's just semantics, but it matters so much. We can't be scared to fail. We have to make mistakes and screw up and admit our failures so that we can learn, improve, and change.

The shortest definition for failure is "lack of success," but that works only if you assume there is one great outcome possible for each project or problem. Your project might not "succeed" in the way that you expected, but did you learn anything? Do you now know something you didn't? What about the accidental result that occurred? Can you build on that?

Of course sometimes failure is awful! Rejection sucks. Going all in on something that doesn't pan out is terrible. I am not asking you to put on some rose-colored glasses and look at that spilled cup of milk as half full. *You get to be mad when things go wrong. But you don't get to not attempt things because they could go wrong.*

Failure is not the end of the world. Instead it's a huge part of being a member of the world.

How change feels

WE ARE LIVING IN a swipe-to-see-the-before-photo world where home transformations take twenty-two minutes and a few commercial breaks. This is often how we see change happen, and so it's not surprising that we want quick results. We want a montage. We want a spectacular "ta-da!" moment.

This, sadly, isn't coming.

Instead, change is hard! And slow! It takes commitment, patience, and effort.

Have you ever lifted weights or gone for a run or moved boxes for a few hours and spent the next day in pain? Yes, of course you have. You also probably are aware that the reason you feel that pain is that in exerting yourself, you've created tiny tears in your muscles that are now working to heal themselves. They will heal stronger, but that doesn't mean this process—the regrowth process—doesn't hurt.

This is what all change is like.

Change is tiny micro-tears that you have to sit with and let heal and then continue to tear and heal over and over again. When you try something new for the first time, it usually feels uncomfortable or strange. *This doesn't mean stop.* This means keep trying.

Pick a mantra to return to

SOMETHING THAT I FIND the most helpful when I am feeling overwhelmed is the phrase *You're okay*. I mutter it when I'm feeling frustrated in traffic. I think it when I'm trying to hold a plank pose or run up a hill. I repeat it when I'm looking at a never-ending list or pile of work that needs to be done. I try to believe it when it's the middle of the night and the girls are sick. I said it to myself on a loop as I prepared to meet my daughters via C-section and basically should have tattooed it on my arm throughout those newborn weeks.

I say it to the girls when they wake up from a bad dream or when they fall and skin their knees. I didn't realize how often I said it until I heard Piper recently comforting her doll in the same soothing tone, "You're okay, baby. You're okay."

I use this mantra as a reminder to take a deep breath. Am I breathing? Yes. Okay. "You're okay." *This is going to be okay.*

What phrase or mantra can you add to your toolbox (please feel free to borrow mine) that will help you get through this? What will give you a quick jolt of perspective and enough patience, courage, or energy to power through? Your mantra won't solve the problem. It won't take away the pain. It will not do the work. But it can serve as a reminder to get back to a clearer headspace.

You're OK, you're OK, this is going to be OK. You're OK, you're OK, this is going to be OK. You're OK, you're OK, this is going to be OK. You're OK, you're OK, this is going to be OK. You're OK, you're OK, this is going to be OK. You're OK, you're OK, this is going to be OK. You're OK, you're OK, this is going to be OK. You're OK, you're OK, this is going to be OK. You're OK, you're OK, this is going to be OK. You're OK, you're OK, this is going to be OK. You're OK, you're OK, this is going to be OK. You're OK, you're OK, this is going to be OK. You're OK, you're OK, this is going to be OK. You're OK, you're OK, this is going to be OK. You're OK, you're OK, this is going to be OK.

Today is
the day

WHAT ARE YOU WAITING FOR? What's keeping you from clearing a bit of space in your week and taking a step toward something bigger? What's holding you back from announcing your plan? What's wrong with starting today? What's going to change dramatically next year or five years from now or ten years from now that's going to make what you're dreaming about possible?

Maybe nothing will be different in ten years. Maybe everything will be different in ten years. But one thing is for sure. You'll have missed out on *ten years* of trying the things you want to try. Don't do that. If you start today and it takes ten years to reach your goal . . . amazing! You're still done early. You've still "finished" before you planned to start.

This is it. Today, for better or worse, is it. What you are doing today is your life's work.

What will your life's work look like? ➨

Now what?

AS I WROTE THIS BOOK, I found myself typing over and over again, "Don't panic." Some of those phrases have been pulled from the final draft because I basically wanted to end each section with "don't panic," but that would have been excessive. When it did appear, I hope when you read it that you took a deep breath.

I have been sharing my life online for a long time. A side effect of oversharing is that I have corresponded with hundreds of people about their various creative ventures and life decisions over the years. The underlying emotion in their emails, comments, and messages is often tinged with fear.

"I have too many ideas and I don't know where to start."

"I just had a baby and I can't see how I'll ever have time for me again."

"I don't know if I should take this job across the country."

"I can't find what is the right thing for me."

"I am nervous to start this project because I don't know how to do step 7."

What most people are looking for is a solution. They want a clear and decisive way out of something or into something, and I know whatever response I type is not going to be enough because it's not going to solve the problem. My answers, by the way:

Don't panic. Pick just one thing for right now. It doesn't even matter which thing— you can draw the idea from a hat and go with it—but just start by taking one step forward on one idea.

Don't panic. I know how hard this is, but I do promise you that it will get better. Things will level out. You will read and walk and cook and talk about something other than the baby and hold extra thoughts in your head and function as you did before. It just takes time.

Don't panic. This job might be the right fit! It could be the best thing for you. But worst-case scenario? It isn't and you have to start over again. At least you'll know.

Don't panic. Finding the right thing is a process. Is there anything right now that feels okay? It doesn't have to feel perfect; just okay will do. Keep doing that for now and continue trying new things on the side. The more you try, the closer you are to finding the right fit.

Don't panic. Focus on step 1 for now. Then, once completed, move on to step 2. By the time you get to step 7, you will have been working with this material for longer and you'll have a better understanding of it. You will be holding your progress and you'll be able to see what you are doing. Step 7 is going to make sense once you get there, but not before.

Aside from the reminder to not panic, these responses all require the person to spend some energy and give it some time. My overarching response is basically a recommendation that you keep going—even if the direction you are going in will need to shift.

Because this, folks, is the point:

You have to get up. You have to do the thing. You have to hop in the ring. You have to continue to show up. You have to allow yourself time to figure it out. I can't promise success or achievement or fame or fortune. I *can* promise that you will appreciate all work done in pursuit of your goals. I can promise that choosing to spend the time you have on the work, hobbies, and relationships that you enjoy is something you will never regret.

Don't panic. You're okay. Go get it.

Acknowledgments

I FEEL LUCKY AND GRATEFUL to have had the opportunity to put my words down on paper. I have spent a lot of time staring at a computer screen and tapping away at the keyboard over the past thirteen years, but this experience felt like the most important. It has been a gift to share my thoughts with you.

Thank you to my agent, Maria Ribas, for your expert guidance and for helping me get paid to write.

Thank you to my editor, Rachel Hiles, for championing my voice and idea at Chronicle.

Thank you to my book designer, Kelley Galbreath, for the layout and design of this book. It's wonderfully whole and complete.

Thank you to my parents, to whom I owe everything. You're my original and forever sounding boards, and without your endless support, encouragement, and wisdom, there would be no book.

Thank you, Paul, for brewing the coffee, understanding my workflow, continuing the conversation, and being my equal partner. You're my favorite and I love you.

Thank you, Ellerie and Piper, for teaching me how to dive deep. My biggest dream and daily joy is to learn alongside you two for the rest of my life.

And thank you, friend, for stumbling on my blog after a Google search, for following a link, for sticking around through the mixed metaphors and spelling errors, for coming over to Instagram, for understanding that I will never check my Facebook messages. I wrote this book for you. The fact that you read and occasionally shared my internet rambling is the only reason why I was given this opportunity. I hope I made you proud. I hope you're inspired to get to work and that you take some time each day to enjoy it.

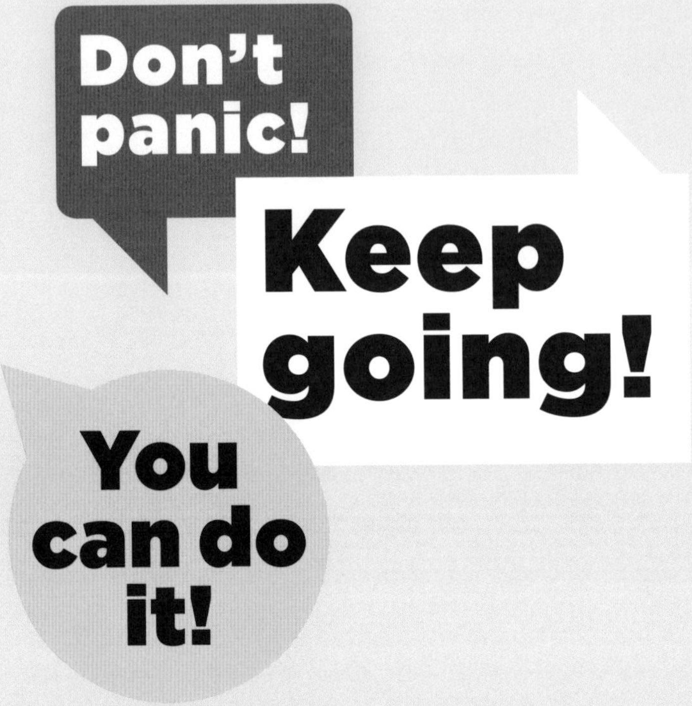
Don't panic!
Keep going!
You can do it!